Fifty Psalms

FIFTY PSALMS

An Attempt at a New Translation

Huub Oosterhuis

Michel van der Plas

Pius Drijvers

Han Renckens

Frans Jozef van Beeck

David Smith

Forrest Ingram

HERDER AND HERDER

1969
HERDER AND HERDER NEW YORK
232 Madison Avenue, New York, N.Y. 10016

Library of Congress Catalog Card Number: 71–80273
Manufactured in the United States

The priests and the levites had to bring up the Ark of the Lord, Israel's God. David set apart for the service a number of men from the clans of Asaph, Heman, and Jeduthun ; they all sang in the house of the Lord under the king's orders and under the direction of their fathers, to the accompaniment of cymbals, harps, and lyres. All of them were trained in singing to the Lord, two hundred aud eighty-eight skilful musicians. Benaiah and Jahaziel, the priests, had to blow the trumpets all the time.

It was on that day that David had the praise of the Lord sung for the first time by Asaph and his brethren :

> "Give thanks to God, for he is good,
> his love endures in eternity."

And the whole people cried : "Amen! Halleluiah!"

And when Solomon had finished building the house of the Lord, a song was raised, with trumpets and cymbals and other instruments :

> "Give thanks to God, for he is good,
> his love endures in eternity."

Then the Lord's house was filled with a dark cloud, so that the priests could not go on with the service, for the glory of the Lord filled the house of the Lord. And Solomon said : "The Lord has chosen to live in clouds and darkness. I have built a lofty house for you, a house to live in for ever. Now, *my God, look down and listen to the prayers heard in this place." At last he let the people go home with joy and gladness in their hearts because they knew that God was good.*

Thus, ever since the days of David, the Man of God, long ago, there have been guilds of singers with their songs of praise and thanksgiving to God.

Contents

Introduction

An attempt is an experiment, a beginning made with a minimum of fixed rules.

When work was first started on the Dutch original of this book, not everything was completely clear, and much more time could have been spent in preliminary discussion. Yet it seemed preferable to get down to business with a provisional method of work, and to try to reach greater clarity while actually working. This clarity in fact came in this way. Thanks to this lack of previous discussion the effort to translate the psalms was not directed against anything or anybody—the collaborators were concerned only with the psalms themselves.

At first many more people were involved in the project and an even wider sphere of collaboration was envisaged. But the need for efficient work and frequent meetings spontaneously led to the formation of a small group of collaborators. The result is that basically only two poets and two scripture-scholars are responsible for the texts in this collection. It is not difficult to guess how the undertaking came about—there was an existing situation and a holy conviction, and the two interacted on each other.

The introduction of the liturgy in the language of the people exposed the painful lack of good texts both for speaking and for singing. The urgent liturgical need was for a strong vernacular that would be both fairly durable and carefully considered by experts from the point of view of sound and rhythm. The content was, of course, even more important, but this was readily available—the psalms express man's existence and his religious experience in such a pure and impressive way that they provide irreplaceable material both for liturgical singing and for personal prayer.

Although the first intention of the collaborators was to provide psalms that could be used in the new liturgy, they also aimed consciously at a much wider sphere of interest and hoped that their fifty psalms would prove suitable in all kinds of situations, including the field of education. This meant that their selection had also to reflect something of the rich variety of the psalter, with the result that at least one typical example was chosen to represent each of the most important kinds of psalm. Weak passages in the translation cannot therefore in themselves and in all cases be attributed to lack of ability on the part of the translators—the original poetry is sometimes itself weak.

In spite of all the initial lack of clarity, then, there was a clear aim at the very outset: the language had to be as good as possible, but not at the expense of the psalms themselves, which had to remain authentically the psalms. This explains why the poets and the exegetes always worked so closely together. Older and more recent translations, both Dutch and foreign, were constantly consulted. These clarified and confirmed the special purpose of the undertaking—after all, why simply do again what has already been done so often and so well? In other words, this attempt at a translation of fifty of the psalms does not make the slightest claim to replace any of the existing translations. After all, it comprises no more than one-third of the psalter. Those who have collaborated in it believe that the result of their work may be of use at an opportune time and place, and that it may possibly also serve as a contribution to a more authentic understanding of the already existing translations.

Within the group of collaborators, the task of the two exegetes was to make clear what the whole range of meaning and expression was in each psalm selected for translation, word by word, verse by verse, and finally in the psalm as a whole. Wherever the text was disputed or corrupt, they had to make a responsible choice or else leave the choice between several possibilities open after giving their reasons for and against. In this way the poets knew the sphere within which they could move, and within this sphere they had then to track down and exploit all the possibilities of form, vocabulary, and idiom in their own language. Their first draft, often very uneven and full of provisional translations and unanswered questions, was then thoroughly discussed together with the exegetes, and a combined search was afterwards made for any possibilities of new meanings in the Hebrew and of new expressions in the vernacular. In this way, an increasing number of psalms came very gradually on the stocks, each psalm, however, in a different stage of construction—some hardly looked at and others entirely or almost completed.

The most difficult aspect of this task, which was at the same time its most fascinating aspect, was that of "translating" the psalmist's world of ideas and experience in such a way that the human and religious content of the psalms could really come across to people of today, and be recognized, prayed, and realized by them. To achieve this, it was impossible simply to translate one word by another. "Words are not coins, dead things whose value can be mathematically computed", as Ronald Knox warns in that delightful by-product of his translation of the Bible, *On Englishing the Bible*. So one association had rather to be "translated" by another. The translators had therefore not only to enter into the psalmist's human situation and religious experience—they had also, and above all, to penetrate into what the psalmist's real intention was within this human and religious experience. In other words, his experience had to be understood simply as the expression of human religiosity determined by conditions of time and place. Once this had been achieved, it was possible to go further and look for a more contemporary expression of the same basic fact.

There was, then, a constant interaction between the exegetes, who looked for indications in the psalms of the Hebrew mode of feeling and expressing human and religious experience with all its echoes and overtones, and the poets, who explored the possibilities of man's contemporary sensibility and modern ways of expressing this. This often led to a common level of contact which really gave access for the first time to a certain word in the psalms.

When the psalms had been published and were being used it occurred to a Dutch theologian who is also an English scholar that the gap between the Hebrew psalms and the Dutch translation had been far more difficult to bridge than the gap between the Dutch translation and an English one would be, not only at the level of meaning and sensibility, but also at the level of poetical form and diction. The translation into English on the basis of the Dutch text actually proved a minor enterprise, compared to the previous process of transformation from Hebrew into Dutch, which the translator was in a position to retrace with the help of the notes made by the exegetes and the drafts made by the poets. Yet, the English translation, whose final text was established in collaboration with an Englishman and an American, both of whom are modern-language scholars who know Dutch, is a translation from the Dutch only in so far as a straightforward rendering of the Dutch text could result in an English text with the same qualities as the Dutch. In many cases, a recourse to the Hebrew text and other English translations was necessary to arrive at an English text which would do justice to the intentions of the authors of the Dutch translation.

It is, of course, to be expected that some people will think that the translations in this collection are not literal enough, and in certain cases they may be right. The translators have probably not always succeeded in replacing a wooden or unintelligible literal version that is no longer meaningful by a freer text which at the same time still goes to the very heart of the matter. Within the framework of their set purpose they had, in these cases, either to translate creatively and therefore fairly audaciously or else not to translate at all. These fifty psalms can justify their existence only in so far as they have been able to avoid the blemishes which are inevitably associated with literal prose translations. What are these blemishes? They are that literal translation not only presents us with a rendering that is, in many cases, open to question, but also that it does not really fulfil its own special purpose. If it is true, in Ronald Knox's words, that "what the reader wants, I insist, is to get the illusion that he is reading, not a translation, but an original work in his own language", then it must be said that *a too literal translation does not do sufficient justice to the original text precisely because it is too literal.* This point deserves to be illustrated by two comments, which, it is hoped, will throw light on the whole situation.

1. The linguistic and stylistic means of ancient Hebrew are different from those of modern European languages such as Dutch or English. Anyone who simply takes over a Hebrew expression is being unfaithful to the datum of the text if the effect of this expression is not conveyed in his own language. The translation is only faithful when the translator uses a vernacular expression which has a similar effect. Thus, parallelism ("the subtlest irritant of all"—Ronald Knox) is a "law" of Hebrew verse, but not of English poetry. If it is reproduced in English, it can have a disturbing and enfeebling effect, whereas, in the original, it was used to strengthen the effect of what was being said. A quotation from the Revised Standard Version reflects very well this Hebrew habit of parallelism. A strong pair of lines is weakened in the modern version, because

the two halves of the verse simply have the effect of pure repetition:

> *I cry with my voice to the Lord,*
> *with my voice I make supplication to the Lord* (Ps. 142. 1).

The repetition, especially that of the name of God, has the effect of simply marking time. The translators of *Fifty Psalms*, on the other hand, making use of all the Hebrew terms and using their fundamental meaning as their inspiration, build up an English climax which very closely approximates the urgency and the fierceness of the original Hebrew:

> *I am crying out, I cry to God—*
> *o God, I implore you and beg for mercy.*

In this way, the parallel elements of this Semitic turn of phrase are linked to each other in a more English manner. In the same way, the well-known phrase from the Revised Standard Version:

> *. . . let the earth rejoice;*
> *let the many coastlands be glad!*   (Ps. 97. 1)

has become in this new translation:

> *all the shores on earth*
> *are laughing and shouting for joy.*

Similarly, all the data of:

> *He makes peace in your borders.*
> *he fills you with the finest of the wheat*   (Ps. 147. 14)

are contained in:

> *He gives you bread and peace—*
> *you live a life of abundance*

in which the sacrifice of a genuinely Hebrew expression is

compensated by a terse phrase which yet evokes the whole of human life and human aspirations. Leaving certain hebraisms out of the translation does not therefore imply an impoverishment. An example of this can be found at the beginning of Psalm 139. In the older translation, the three hebraisms are reproduced thus:

> *Thou knowest when I sit down and when I rise up, . . .*
> *Thou searchest out my path and my lying down,*
> *and art acquainted with all my ways.*

In the present translation, they appear as follows:

> *My God, you know where I am, where I go. . . .*
> *you have decided my roaming and resting,*
> *and you are familiar with all that I do.*

The "law" of parallelism imposes on Hebrew verse an excessive use of closely synonymous words such as God and Yahweh, soul and spirit, praise and bless, rejoice and exult, sea and water, ways and paths, and so on. These regularly recurring tautologies do not by any means always arise from poetic necessity, with the result that they frequently occur in places where the inner tension of the poem does not require them at all. The collection of *Fifty Psalms* had therefore to be sometimes more concise and sometimes more detailed. It is, for example, more concise in Psalms 8. 3; 22. 24, 26; 24. 1, 5, and elsewhere, and more detailed, by means of a kind of resolution into factors, for example, in Psalms 23. 5 and 97. 4. In this latter psalm, the older versions had

> *the earth sees and trembles*

or a similar phrase. But this really does not express any of the strength of the description, in Hebrew, of the theophany—it just does not make it. The original Hebrew, however, is very powerful, because "tremble" is the technical term for "labour", the pangs of childbirth, and a favourite image for eschatological terror (cf. Is. 13. 8; 26. 17; Jer. 4. 31; 6. 24; Ps. 48. 7; 1 Thess. 5. 3). The translators therefore felt that it was necessary to charge the word "tremble" with special meaning, not by trying to make something of it, but by drawing on the biblical echo contained in it—that of the pain of a woman in childbirth. Their version thus reads:

> *The whole of the world has seen it.*
> *The earth was writhing and groaning*
> *like a woman in labour.*

This is, of course, an extreme example. It does not lend itself to systematic application, but it does illustrate what was involved in the translation.

2. Many Hebrew terms have a different range of meaning and evoke associations which are quite different from, and often much richer than, those evoked by the traditional translations of these terms. Biblicisms such as "justice" (also one of Ronald Knox's cruxes: cf. *On Englishing the Bible*, pp. 11, 30–4) and "fearing the Lord" certainly evoke a mistaken image, unless one has learnt to understand them precisely as biblicisms. But the whole purpose of the translation was to make the psalms accessible to those who do not belong to the elect group of those who are familiar with biblical language. It was here especially that the translators had to seek out new paths if they were to avoid doing essentially superfluous work. Terms, images, and expressions which have a different function or which do not function at all in modern English or in contemporary human experience had to be fathomed for their full range of meaning and their actual meaning in the text, before an equivalent that does function now could be sought.

How far-reaching that task was can be gathered from a summary and incomplete list of such words. Firstly, some which relate to God: holiness, glory, face, Yahweh (Lord), name, justice, mercy, peace, salvation, right hand, law, ways, judgment. Secondly, some relating to man: the saints, the godly, those who fear God, the upright in heart, the righteous, the blameless, the pure, the poor, the humble, the lowly, the afflicted, the sinners, the wicked, the scoffers, those who do violence, the strangers. And thirdly, some that are of a more psychological nature: heart, soul, spirit, "reins", truth, vanity, deceit, knowing, confessing, praising, exalting, extolling, and putting to shame. The beginning of Ps. 103 in the Revised Standard Version may serve as an example:

> Bless the Lord, O my soul;
> and all that is within me,
> bless his holy name!
> Bless the Lord, O my soul,
> and forget not all his benefits.

The very first word, "bless", already presents us with a difficulty, because it is no longer very much alive in modern English. What is more, its real meaning is: to pronounce a blessing, which to Hebrew ears means: to state and enumerate in detail and to extol—hence "to praise", which is what the psalm in fact goes on to do.

The word "soul" is also very difficult. In Hebrew it is intense and meaningful, but it hardly needs to be said that it is weak in English. The word "soul", however, still continues to function in such expressions as "heart and soul" and "deep down in my soul". The translators have therefore tried to find a solution in this direction. How the rest of the opening of this psalm came about will be sufficiently clear from the result. Every line has a metre of four stressed syllables:

> I want to call him by his Name,
> the holy God, as truly as I live.
> I thank him from the bottom of my heart,
> and I will forget none of his benefits.

This is, of course, in no sense a literal translation, but it is better than the older translations in two ways—the pathos of the original Hebrew is conveyed more clearly and the idiom is better. Just imagine the first two lines being sung as a refrain, and then compare the two versions.

The original Dutch edition of these fifty psalms does not contain a single word of comment or explanation. The psalms can indeed be left to speak for themselves, but the book was still felt to be a bit merciless. Moreover, if the book of psalms is really—to quote St Thomas Aquinas—the whole of the Old Testament in the form of prayer, it was felt that a collection of psalms like the present one could be turned into a prayerful (and therefore unsystematical) introduction to the Old Testament, offering knowledge in the only framework in which knowledge can be fruitful—experience. The commentaries, various as they are, are designed to give this extra purpose to the book, which means that they must be ignored if they are felt to be in the way of the psalms themselves.

For the psalms speak for themselves, reveal what the collaborators have done with the text, and, on closer comparison, give some indication of the frequently laborious paths and detours which had to be followed before a given text acquired its present form. It is an attempt. This presupposes the possibility of better discoveries. Note them down.

Fifty Psalms

Psalm 1

Happy is the man
who does not seek advice from godlessness,
who does not set his foot in the ways of evil,
who will not sit in circles where they laugh
at God and at his law.
Happy is that man—
he seeks with all his heart the word of God,
and savours words of wisdom night and day.

He is a tree, planted near living water,
he always bears good fruit.
And he will never wilt before his time—
whatever he undertakes will thrive.

But unhappy those people who despise God's word;
they are like chaff, blown away on the wind.
They will not keep their foothold in the judgment,
when he assembles all his righteous friends.

God knows his people and he keeps their ways.
Whoever despises him loses himself.

[Psalm 1] When the different collections of psalms were finally brought together and edited around 300 or 250 B.C., Psalm 1 was added to the collection by way of a general preface. What with its emphasis on the Law and its oracular tone in the vein of the Jewish wisdom-tradition, it is a typically Jewish meditation, impersonal, moralistic, and a bit conventional. The prophetic tone of Joshua 1. 7–9 and especially Jeremiah 17. 5–8 has been formalized to suit the demands of "organized religion". Yet, for the Jew the word *torah* continued to convey more than our present concept of "Law". It also represented "instruction", an introduction to a personal awareness of the fundamental risks and demands of life.—"Go in through the narrow doorway. For the road to perdition is wide and easy, and there are many who take it. But the road to life is narrow and the way to it difficult, and there are only few that discover it" (Matt. 7. 13–14).

Psalm 4

Give me an answer,
God, when I call to you.

You are my truth,
you give me freedom
when I am oppressed—
have mercy on me,
hear my prayer.

Man, how long
will your heart remain hardened,
will you go for appearances
and run after lies?

Do you not know
that God has a friend,
that he makes him great,
and so—that he listens
if I call to him?

Admit defeat
and sin no more,
brand it on your mind
before you sleep,
come to yourself.

Bring your gifts
just as you are,
put your trust
in our God.

Many are asking:
"Who makes us happy?"
Bless us with
the light of your eyes,
Lord our God.

You have given me
greater joy
than all those others
with their riches,
wheat and wine.

In peace I lie down
and I sleep at once.
You make me live
safe and sound, Lord
God, you alone.

[Psalm 4] An evening prayer for reliance and assurance in the form of a quasi-dialogue, taking into account an audience of people who also experience the struggle for faith. The background of this type of self-encouragement lies in the ancient administration of justice in a sacral and cultic setting (cf., e.g., 1 Kings 8. 31 ff.). Here, this background has been given new life by casting it into the form of an invitation, addressed to the believer by the Wise Man, to appeal to God and surrender to him, as a man would surrender to sleep after the day's struggles are over.—"Make yourselves humble under God's powerful hand: He will relieve you in his own good time. Confide all your anguish to him, for he cares for you" (1 Peter 5. 6–7).

Psalm 8

Lord our Lord, how powerful is your Name
everywhere on earth.

You show your majesty in the heavens,
yet you open the mouths of helpless children,
and there rises a song that bewilders your enemy—
all your opponents are put to silence.

If I look at the heavens, the work of your fingers,
the moon and the stars which you set in place—
what, then, is Man, that you remember him,
the son of Adam, that he touches your heart.

Yet you have made him almost a god,
and you have crowned him with glory and splendour.
You make him lord of the work of your hands,
and you have laid the whole world at his feet,

sheep and cattle, all, all things,
even the animals in the open plain,
the birds of the air, the fish of the sea,
all that wanders on the paths of the water.

Lord our Lord, how powerful is your Name
everywhere on earth.

[Psalm 8] Israel has always marvelled at the humanity of her God. All the gods of her neighbours were associated with the irresistible forces of Nature and the World, which left to Man no attitudes but those of cowering fear or arrogant collusion. But from the first chapter of Genesis onward the Bible presents Adam and his children, in spite of all their weakness, as never at the mercy of "the powers", but on the contrary, always above them. God is not the Lord of creation at the expense of Man. He is not a Moloch, but the God of Mankind, and "serving him is reigning" (St Leo the Great). At the basis of Israel's belief in God is the conviction that power is not the key to life, but service and love, which are stronger than the powers, even the powers of death and destruction. Our God has displayed the height of his power in the faithful and humble Servant (cf. Is. 42), "in Christ, by raising him up from the dead and by making him sit at his right hand in the heavens, high above all authorities, powers, forces and dominions, and above all that deserves a name both in this world and beyond it; and 'he has laid the whole world at his feet'. And God has made him the Head of the Church, his body; and thus he is the full realization of all creation" (Eph. 1. 20–23).

Psalm 11

My shelter is with him.

Why, then, say to me:
"Bird, flee into the mountains.
There, that man without God
bends his bow and takes aim,
shoots in the night, will strike
the heart of innocence.
If the foundations are crumbling,
what is the use of goodness?"

God, in his holy house,
he, on his throne in heaven,
seeks the world with his eyes,
tests the children of Adam.

He sees through the good and the wicked,
and whole-heartedly, he
detests those who breed terror.
He rains on their kind
showers of fire and sulphur;
a scorching desert-wind is
what they get for their thirst.

He, the true God himself,
he loves justice and truth.
Innocence will live to see him.

[Psalm 11] The social world of Israel offered two alternatives to somebody who was persecuted: he could either make use of the right of asylum, or he had to leave everything behind and go into hiding in the mountains, the abode of the outlaws and the victims of power. But where is the just man to go if he finds that "the whole earth is filled with violence" (Gen. 6. 13)? The psalmist says: ultimately we are faced with the choice between a panicky flight from the world and the surrender of faith. Faith and trust are in the end the only cure for the uncertainty brought about by the kind of demoralization described, for example, in Isaiah 59. 3–8. The psalmist does not believe in violence against violence, no more than the suffering Servant, who "had done no violence" (Is. 53. 9). Again, the key to life is not grabbing for power, but the faithful distinction between "the Lord loves" and "the Lord detests", the anticipations of the later concepts of Heaven and Hell.—"What, then, shall we say? If God is for us, who will be against us? Will the God who did not spare his own Son but gave him up for us all not also give us everything with him? Who shall bring any charge against God's chosen people? If God gives justice, who can condemn?" (Rom. 8. 31–34).

Psalm 19

I

The heavens unfold the glory of God,
the firmament boasts of the work of his hands.
The day hands it on to the following day,
the nights tell each other of what they know.
There is no speaking, there are no words,
and their voices are not to be heard—
and yet their rhythm is everywhere felt,
their echo reaches the edge of the earth.

There he has pitched a tent for the sun—
a bridegroom leaving the bridal chamber,
a hero that shouts for joy on his way,
that is the sun—he climbs along the skies
and goes down again at the farthest horizon,
and nothing can hide itself from his heat.

II

The word of the Lord is perfect,
source of life.
Our God's witness is trustworthy—
unwisdom grows wise.

Limpid water is his law,
refreshing our hearts.
His commandments: right and reason,
light to our eyes.

What he promises is pure truth,
only peace.
What he does is all done well,
everlasting.

And as exquisite as honey,
no, still more—
far more precious than pure gold
is the Lord's own word.

III

You will be worth all our trouble
if we keep your word, o Lord.
But who knows the ways of his heart?
Free us from our secret evil.

Let us not be the slaves of pride,
preserve your people from conceit.
Let us not break with you, God,
but go to meet you without fear.

All the words we speak to you,
all we think within our hearts
may find grace with you, my God,
with you, my rock and my redeemer.

[Psalm 19] This magnificent psalm is a liturgical composition, consisting of a hymn to God the Creator, a meditative praise of the Law, and a prayer for purity of heart and faith in God. It may have been used in the Temple at the time of the morning sacrifice, which celebrated the rising sun as the symbol of justice and the giving of the Law on Mount Sinai. Israel, conscious of having God's eternal mercy and wisdom dwelling in her midst in the shape of the *Torah*, the Law (cf. Sirach 24. 3-12), does not cower under "the frightening silence of those infinite spaces" (Pascal); on the contrary, their very silence has become eloquent to the People of God.—"In the beginning was the Word, and the Word was with God, and the Word was God. He was in the beginning with God; all things were made through him, and nothing of all that was made was made without him. (. . .) And the Word became flesh and dwelt among us, full of mercy and faithfulness, and we have seen his glory. (. . .) And from his fulness we have all received, mercy after mercy. For the Law was given through Moses; mercy and faithfulness have come through Jesus, the Christ. No one has ever seen God, but the only Son, who is in the bosom of the Father, he has been our guide" (John 1. 1-3, 14, 16-18).

Psalm 22

1

God, my God, why have you abandoned me?
I cry out, and you stay far away.
"My God", I call all day—you are silent,
I call through the night, and you just let me call.

O you, most holy God, enthroned
in the place where Israel's songs are sung,
our fathers put all their trust in you,
they trusted and you have been their rescue.
They called for you and you were their way out,
and never have you disappointed their trust.

But I am no longer a man but a worm,
scorned by men, despised by my neighbours.
I am a mockery in everyone's eyes,
all of them laugh at me, shaking their heads—
"He held on to the Lord, then let him deliver him,
let the God that so loves him come to his rescue."

Was it not you who drew me from the womb
and made me rest at the breast of my mother?
At birth I was put in the hollow of your hands,
you are my God from my mother's womb onward.
And why should you now be so far away?
I am close to despair, there is no one to help.

II

A savage crowd bears down upon me,
lumbering bulls press in from all sides,
they open wide their jaws to me,
ravenous lions are roaring for prey.

I am poured out, wasted like water,
and my bones are out of joint.
My soul in me is melted away,
my heart is torn from within me.

Dry as burnt clay is my throat
and my tongue sticks to my palate.
They force me down into the dust of death,
they are unleashing their hounds at me.

The mob has gathered all around me
and they have pierced my hands and feet.
One by one, I can count my ribs.
They are looking on and enjoying it.

They divide my clothes among each other,
and they gamble for my cloak.
And you, my God, you are so far away—
will you not help me, are you not my strength?

Do not surrender me to the sword,
do not give me up to the power of those dogs.
Save my life from the jaws of the lion,
me, poor man, from the horns of the bulls.

III

I will tell my brothers about him,
hold up his Name in the midst of the gathering—
"Sons of Israel, people of God,
you must worship him full of awe.
Never has he scorned the poor for being poor,
never has he turned his back upon me,
nor avoided me, but heard my cries."

This is my song in the heart of the gathering,
and there I shall fulfil my promise.
The poor, they shall eat and have their fill,
and all who look for him bless his Name.
They will come to life for ever and ever.

The ends of the earth will remember it,
and turn round to meet this God.
And all generations of all mankind
will one day bend their knees before him.
For to him belong the power and the kingdom,
he is the Lord of races and nations.
And even those who lie down in the dust
and no longer live shall worship him.

But I will live with heart and soul.
My children will also be there to serve him,
and speak about him to their children, too.
All who are yet to be born after us
will come to hear it: our God is faithful.
It is the Lord who has done all this.

[Psalm 22] The basic structure of this psalm is that of a complaint of someone wrongly persecuted, followed by a hymn of thanksgiving for the hoped-for deliverance. But the violence of the complaint as well as the large scope of the thanksgiving have given this psalm a much broader significance. Thus it became, together with chapters 52–53 in Isaiah, to which it bears a strong resemblance, one of the classical texts used by the Christian tradition to bear witness to the redeeming passion of Jesus. The synoptic Gospels have Jesus say the first line of this psalm on the cross, and the synoptic accounts of the passion allude to the first two sections several times. The last section, with its liturgical overtones, puts the past sufferings of the just man in a universalist perspective, so that the Christian tradition has also come to look upon this psalm as a prophetic witness to the resurrection of Christ and to the offer of salvation to all mankind.—"It was fitting that God, the Creator and End of all things, should bring the pioneer of all his children that were to be saved to perfection through suffering. For those who are sanctified by Christ have the same common origin as Christ, who is the source of their sanctification. And that is why he is not ashamed of calling them his brothers: "I will tell my brothers about him, hold up his Name in the midst of the gathering"" (Heb. 2. 10–12).

Psalm 23

My shepherd is the Lord,
I shall never want for anything.

He takes me to an oasis of green—
there I stretch out at the edge of the water,
where I find rest.
I come to life again, then we go forward
along trusted roads—he leads the way.
For God is his Name.

Although I must enter the darkness of death,
I am not anxious since you are with me—
in your keeping I dare to do it.

You invite me to sit at your table,
and all my enemies, with envious eyes,
have to look on while you wait upon me,
while you anoint me, my skin and my hair,
while you fill up my cup to the brim.

Happiness and mercy are coming to meet me
everywhere, every day of my life.
And always I go back to the house
of the Lord, as long as I live.

[Psalm 23] Ever since Abraham set out on his journey (Gen. 12. 1–4), faith in God, according to Scripture, has been, not an entrenched position, but a "Way" (Acts 9. 2). And for the "wandering Arameans" (Deut. 26. 5) the notion of journeying was inextricably bound up with the life of the nomadic shepherd, leading his family and his flock with unremitting faithfulness (Hebrew: *emet*, truth) from one oasis to another, from one pasture to another. No wonder, then, that these straying people, always strangers wherever they were, developed a nostalgia for a promised land where life would be without any further travelling. It is against this background that this beautiful psalm was composed, and that, for example, the prophet Ezechiel (34) came to describe God as the shepherd, faithfully leading his people to Life along his own ways. The mention of the table also points to a cultic background, also suggested by the meal on Mount Sinai (Exod. 24. 11) during Israel's journey through the desert; this has been taken up by the Christian tradition, which has applied this psalm to Baptism and the Eucharist.—"I am the good shepherd. The good shepherd gives up his life for his sheep." "I am the Way, the Truth, and the Life. Nobody comes to the Father except through me" (John 10. 11; 14. 6).

Psalm 24

The earth is the Lord's, his is this world
and those who live in it. He by himself
built it on the streams and anchored it safely.

Who may climb to the height of God,
who has the run of his holy city?
People with no guilt on their hands.

People with hearts that have been cleansed,
who do not build their lives on appearances,
who will not forge lies against others.

They find comfort and blessing with him,
they are the kind that look for God,
that want to see him, with their own eyes.

Gates, lift up and raise your heads,
reach up higher, you everlasting doors—
here comes the king of glory.

Who is the king of glory?
It is the Lord, the powerful and strong One,
it is the Lord, the strong One in battle.

Gates, lift up and raise your heads,
reach up higher, you everlasting doors—
here comes the king of glory.

Who is he, the king of glory?
He is our God, the Lord of the powers,
he is the king of glory.

[Psalm 24] This psalm is a liturgical composition consisting of several elements. The end is formed by an old processional hymn, celebrating God as the protector of his people in the holy war (*Yahweh Sebaot*, Lord of the powers, the armies); this part may go back to the days when the Ark as the symbol of God's presence accompanied the people on its expeditions, to be victoriously carried back to the sanctuary after the battle (cf. 2 Sam. 6. 1–19 for a prototypical description of this). The middle part is a liturgy at the gates of the Temple, incorporating an instruction, in the mouth of the priest, about the virtues required to take part in the cult, whereas the opening lines declare that the God of Israel's rescue and of personal salvation is also the Creator of the world. From these very different elements the psalm builds up a meditation on the discovery of God's presence through a humble search and purity of heart.—"Blessed are the pure in heart, for they will see God" (Matt. 5. 8).

Psalm 25

My desire goes out to you.

Lord, my God, I am certain of you—
and would you ever let me down,
will my enemies carry the day?
No, you will never put us to shame,
all those people who wait for you.
But those who recklessly break with you,
they will be put to shame.

Make me, Lord, at home in your ways,
lead me, put me on the track of your truth.
Guide me, you are the God who saves me,
I am waiting for you as long as I live.
Have you not always been good to me,
merciful love, from the very beginning?
Forget then, Lord, the sins of my youth,
and if I broke faith, do not remember.
Think of me only with love and mercy.

God is good and no deceiver,
He shows straight ways to those who are lost.
And to poor and humble people
he gives the strength to go his way.
All he does is love and trust,
for all who keep his covenant alive,
for all who hold on to his word.

For the sake of your Name, forgive me—
you alone can forgive my guilt.

Let a man hold God in honour—
he will know what ways to go.
He will find happiness and life,
his sons will receive the earth to themselves.
God will take him into his trust
and guide him into his covenant.
My eyes are always looking for him,
he lifts me up when I have fallen.

Take notice of me and show your mercy,
for I am lonely, with no one to help.
My heart is anxious and oppressed—
open me, give me space and freedom.

Do not turn away from my misery,
take my sins away from me.
Surely you know that I have enemies
who hate me with a deadly hatred?
Rescue me from their hands, Lord God,
or will you put my trust to shame?

May simple uprightness always keep me,
for I wait for you as long as I live.

Come and free us from our anguish.

[Psalm 25] In the Hebrew original this psalm is an alphabetic poem: the first letters of the lines follow the Hebrew alphabet. The result is a patchwork of standard formulas adding up to a prayer interrupted by lines of Jewish wisdom and covering a number of concepts and attitudes going back to very different layers of the Old Testament tradition: the Covenant, the sufferings at the hands of (pagan) enemies, awareness of sin and prayer for repentance and salvation, "the way" after the fashion of Deuteronomy and the Wisdom books, and the frame of mind of the *anawim*, the poor of the Lord, who await their rescue from oppression from God alone. The surprising feature of this psalm, however, is its unity of atmosphere, which shows how all the major elements of the variegated tradition of the Old Testament were eventually fused in the spirituality, at once simple and full of ardour, of the pious Jews after the period of exile, a few centuries B.C.—"This is also the witness of the holy Spirit to us. For first he says: 'This is the covenant I will make with them one day, says the Lord; I put my laws in their hearts, I stamp them on their minds.' And then: 'I will no longer remember their sins and their evil acts.' But where these are forgiven there is no need for a propitiating sacrifice any more. Therefore, brothers and sisters, we may confidently go up to God's holy place in virtue of the blood of Jesus, by the new and living way which he inaugurated for us through the temple-veil of his own body" (Heb. 10. 15-20).

Psalm 30

I will speak of you, God,
and everyone may hear it:
You have drawn me up,
You have spared me the unholy
glee of all my enemies.
I called to you: "God, help me"—
and you came to heal me.
It was you who brought me back
from the deepest pit—already
I was numbered among the dead—
you have given me life again.

Sing to the Lord our God,
all you that share in his love.
Keep it alive in your songs
that he is the holy One.
His anger is but for a moment,
his friendship lasts a lifetime—
the evening comes with sorrow,
the daybreak brings you gladness.

I was carefree and happy,
I thought: it will ever be so,
I stand, and I will not fall.
And I was not aware
that nothing but your mercy
keeps me alive, Lord God.
And so, when you turned away
from me, I was nowhere.

Then I called out to you, God,
and I begged you for mercy—

"What use is it to you if I die,
if I am laid in the grave?
Can you be praised by the dust,
can a dead man sing of your faithfulness?
So in your goodness hear me, Lord,
be merciful to me and help me."

Then you changed my sorrow
into joy—I was in mourning
and you clothed me with gladness.
And now, with all my heart,
I sing this song to you,
I may no more be silent,
and therefore, God, my God,
I give you endless thanks.

[Psalm 30] Psalm 30 is a classical example of the psalm of praise as a literary kind: the praise of God consists in elaborately and repeatedly recounting, for everybody to hear, the former distress and the rescue from it, accompanied by an appeal to join the psalmist in recognizing God's saving presence. The poet of Psalm 30 has come to realize what it means to come to life and to exist. As the Hebrew title of this psalm indicates, this psalm was sung during the annual feast of the dedication of the Temple: Israel as a whole then celebrated her coming to life as a religious community. The Christian tradition has always prayed this psalm as a confession of Christ's resurrection from the dead.—"We, too, believe, and that is why we speak up. For we know that God, who raised the Lord Jesus from the dead, will also raise us up together with Jesus and bring us with you into his presence. For all this is done for your sake, so that God's grace extends to more and more people, and thanksgiving abounds to the glory of God. No, we do not lose heart. Even though we perish outwardly, our inner life is being renewed every day" (2 Cor. 4. 13–16).

Psalm 32

Happy is the man
whose unfaithfulness is forgiven,
whose evil is forgotten.
What a blessing for him if his sins
do not count any more with God,
if he dares admit:
I have sinned.

As long as I was deaf to
the voice of my own conscience,
I was inwardly eaten up,
I took refuge in self-pity.
Your hand weighed heavily on me,
long days and nights.
My strength was wasting away,
just as a man wastes away
under the heat of summer.

But then I could no longer
hide my evil from you.
I thought: I will go to him
and tell him what I have done—
and you forgave my sin.

And therefore every man
who puts faith in your Name
may go to you with trust
while you let yourself be found.
And should a flood break loose,
he will come to no harm—
as you have allayed my fears,
as you have been yourself
the ark of my salvation.
The song of your redemption
surrounds me everywhere.

II

Word of the Lord your God:
"I will show you the way,
my counsel is for the taking,
I follow you with my eyes.
Man, do not be senseless
and headstrong like a mule,
a horse that has to be
curbed with bit and bridle—
it would go hard with you."

Avoid your God and find
misery where you go;
but admit defeat
and he is merciful.
People of good will,
he is a source of joy—
rejoice, then, be glad in him
with hearts that have been cleansed.

[Psalm 32] Psalm 32, traditionally listed as one of the so-called penitential psalms, was the favourite psalm of St Augustine. It is not so much a penitential prayer as a hymn of thanksgiving, looking back on penance and forgiveness, and turning a personal experience into a passionate appeal to others. A person who tries to run away from his conscience—which means that he is trying to hide from God—will suffer grave distress of conscience, until he stops deluding himself and admits the truth. Relieved and thankful and certain that all is forgiven, the poet warns others that resisting the grace of conscience is a dead end.—"The younger son gathered all he had and left for a distant country, where he squandered his property in loose living. (. . .) But when he came to himself he thought: 'All my father's day-labourers have food enough and to spare, and I am starving. I will go back to my father and say to him: Father, I have sinned against heaven and against you; I am no longer worthy of being called your son.' (. . .) But while he was still at a distance his father saw him; he was moved by pity and came running to meet him. (. . .) 'My son was dead and he has come to life again; he was lost and he has been found again'" (Luke 15. 13, 17–18, 20, 24).

Psalms 42-43

I

As a deer yearns for living water, God,
so do I long with all my heart to go to you.
I thirst for God, the living God—
when will I be at last face to face with my God?
I have no bread but tears, night and day,
and always I hear them saying: "Where is your God?"

I cannot help remembering—and my heart is moved again—
how I went among the throng, to the house of the Lord our God—
then I hear them singing again, all that festive band of people.

But why so discouraged,
why rebellious?
I will wait for God
and one day I shall thank him—
you are my safety, Lord,
you are my God.

II

I am broken-hearted, I think of you
here in the highlands of Jordan and Hermon,
far away from your holy mountain.

Waterfall roars on waterfall here,
voice of your streams—
all your breakers are dashing against me,
waves are sweeping over me.

God, give me to-day and every day
a sign of love, then I will sing to you
till far into the night, as long as I live.

Why, living God, have you forgotten me?
My rock, why do I go about in rags,
harassed and abased?
My enemies drive me to death, body and bones,
I hear them calling: "Where is this God of yours?"

But why so discouraged,
why rebellious?
I will wait for God
and one day I shall thank him—
you are my safety, Lord,
you are my God.

III

God, take up my cause and fight for me
against a godless people that knows no mercy,
save me from the grip of cunning and lies.

For you are my God and my strength—
why did you ever throw me out,
why do I go about in rags,
harassed and abased?

Send out your light and your trust to meet me.
They lead the way to your holy mountain,
they will take me into your house.

Then I may go to the altar of God,
to him, my joy from my earliest years.
Then I shall thank you singing to the harp,
my Lord and my God.

But why then so discouraged,
why rebellious?
I will wait for God
and one day I shall thank him—
you are my safety, Lord,
you are my God.

[Psalms 42–43] Psalms 42 and 43 are looked upon by a long tradition as one psalm, which marks the beginning of a fresh group of psalms, covering books two and three of the present psalter. The first seven (42–49) of this second group are attributed by the Hebrew original to the "sons of Korah", as are Psalms 84, 85, 87, and 88; they may have been a school of singers and poets who considered themselves the heirs of a particular tradition going back to the temple cult of the days of David (cf. 1 Chron. 6. 31, 37). The psalms of the Korah tradition are in any case among the finest literary products of the psalter.—Ostensibly, this psalm is the complaint of a Jew, perhaps a Levite, in exile, who feels that his faith is shaken because he misses the experience of God's presence in the common worship in the Temple at Jerusalem now destroyed by foreign and pagan invaders. But the fact that the third part of the psalm uses the literary convention of the complaint of the man wrongly persecuted suggests that in the last resort this prayer reflects the hankering after God of every believer: "We are always full of courage and aware that while we are at home in the body we are far away from the Lord. (For we lead our lives in faith, and we do not see.) We are, I say, full of courage, and we would rather be away from the body to be at home with the Lord. And thus our only ambition, whether at home or away, is to please him" (2 Cor. 2. 6–9).

Psalm 46

God is our refuge and our strength,
always in adversity he is our help.
Therefore—though the earth should change,
we shall not fear. And let the mountains
tumble and fall deep into the sea,
and let the water foam and rage,
assault the cliffs to set them rocking—

He is for us the God of the powers,
a safe stronghold, a God of men.

I saw a stream of living water,
a stream of joy that branches out
through the city of the Most High.
There he lives—it will stand firm.
His rescue dawns like the morning light.
Kingdoms are tottering, they will fall,
nations are scared and filled with panic,
and the whole world comes crashing down,
when he raises his powerful voice.

He is for us the God of the powers,
a safe stronghold, a God of men.

Come and see, you will stand in awe
of the powerful things he will do on earth:
he puts an end to all war in the world,
shatters the bow, breaks spears into splinters,
throws our weapons into the fire.
He says: "Stop, for I am your God,
I will show myself to all nations,
I will make my Name felt on earth."

He is for us the God of the powers,
a safe stronghold, a God of men.

PSALM 46

[Psalm 46] This psalm, the first of three Korahitic ones celebrating God's presence among his people on Mount Zion (46-48), is a solemn liturgical proclamation of the ultimate power of God, who is at the same time "the God of Jacob", i.e. of Israel, "of men", as the present translation puts it. The first part evokes a kind of inverted creation: the separation of the inhabitable earth from the waters of chaos (Gen. 1. 9) is cancelled again. The third part evokes a totally different perspective: the perfection of creation, the perfection of order, not only in Nature, but also among men. And wedged in between these two extremes stands the experience that leads the celebrating community to hope for the latter perspective in the teeth of the possibility of the former: the experience of the life-giving presence of God in the midst of his people, symbolized by the stream (cf. the powerful evocation in Ezech. 47. 1–12; Is. 8. 3), in which the waters of chaos have been turned into a source of life, just as the streams of Eden watered Paradise (Gen. 2. 10) and the circuit brought the water from the Gihon spring into Jerusalem, the city of peace (cf. 2 Kings 20. 20; Is. 22. 11).—"On the last day of the feast, the great day, Jesus stood up and proclaimed: 'If anyone is thirsty, let him come to me; he may drink, if he believes in me.' As the Scripture says: 'Streams of living water will flow out of his heart.' And in saying this he was referring to the Spirit, which those who were to believe in him would receive" (John 7. 37–39; cf. Apoc. 22. 1).

Psalm 51

Be merciful to me, you who are mercy,
wipe out my guilt, in your compassion.
Wash me, I am dirty with sin—
who can forgive but you alone?

I see the evil that I have done,
it is all around me on every side.
Against your holiness I have sinned,
I have done what is hateful to you.
Your word justly sentences me,
you are righteous.

In unrighteousness I was born,
I was conceived and carried in sin.
Now you want me to come to the truth,
I hear your voice, God, in my conscience.

Cover my sins and wash me clean,
and I shall be as white as snow.
Speak your saving word to me,
you have broken me, you can heal me.
Close your eyes, then, to my sins,
let them no longer exist for you.

Give me a different heart, my God,
make me new and make me firm.
Do not turn away, do not reject me,
never take your holy spirit from me.
Save me, and I can again be happy,
and I dare to live freely again.
Let me be a sign of your mercy,
and all who have disowned you, God,
will find the courage to go back to you.

Hold me no longer a captive of dumbness,
or must I be silent about your mercy?
Put the right words into my mind
to bear witness to your forgiveness.

You want no gifts and sacrifices.
If only, broken and made humble,
if only I open my heart to you,
that is my sacrifice. Lord, accept it.

[In your mercy be good to Zion,
build Jerusalem up again.
Then you will again be pleased with our gifts,
bulls will be offered and burnt on your altar.]

[Psalm 51] Although the formal structure of this famous psalm is that of the prayer for rescue addressed to God by an innocent man (cf. Ps. 22), its novelty is in the fact that the usual protestations of innocence have been replaced by a confession of sinfulness. In this way, the fundamental inspirations of the great prophets, notably Isaiah and Ezechiel, are brought to bear on the problem of persecution and suffering: the loss of peace and worship and prestige can lead the believer to search his own heart. There he may discover the enemy inside (cf. Is. 59. 1–12), and he will wish to be inwardly renewed, to be given a new heart (cf. Ezech. 11. 9), to discover the truth inside so that cult and prestige will no longer rank first as signs of God's blessing. No wonder, then, that the Hebrew Bible attributes this psalm to David at the height of his splendour, and yet repenting of having taken Uriah's wife and driven Uriah himself to death (2 Sam. 11–12). The final lines between brackets, which somehow contradict the passage immediately preceding, were added to justify the cult restored in Jerusalem after the period of the great captivity.—"The woman said to Jesus: 'Lord, I see that you are a prophet. But our fathers used to worship on this mountain, and you Jews say that Jerusalem is the place where people should worship.' Jesus said to her: 'Woman, believe me, the hour comes when neither on this mountain nor in Jerusalem you will worship the Father. (. . . .) The hour comes, and it has already come, when the true worshippers will worship the Father in spirit and truth. God is spirit, and those who worship him must worship in spirit and truth'" (John 4. 19–24).

Psalm 63

God, my God, I look for you.
All I am is thirst for you.
My body is a land without water,
exhausted with desire for you.

I have seen you in your holy house,
with my own eyes, your power and your light.
I know it—your love is more than life.
I wish to praise you as long as I live.

I stretch out my hands to you,
I call your Name—you are my God,
my daily bread, life in abundance—
I will never tire of singing of you.

Night after night you keep me awake,
waking and dreaming I think of you—
always till now you have been my help,
close to you is where I am happy.

You have bound me on your back,
you hold me tight with both your hands.
All those who seek to take my life
perish in the hollow of the earth.

They will fall, die by the sword,
they will be a prey to wild animals.
But I will live and be glad in you,
those who recognize you may speak—

liars will have their big mouths stopped.

[Psalm 63] This is what the experience of a real liturgy can do for a man. The Temple liturgy has brought home to the poet of this psalm who God is, and who he is himself. The experiences of emptiness and fullness, distance and closeness, exhaustion and life, near-despair and profound trust go hand in hand if a man, carried on the waves of common worship, discovers his deepest and most fundamental aspirations, expresses them in words at once too big and too vulnerable, and finally comes out with the Name for it: "You are my God".

> "Thou art lightning and love, I found it, a winter and warm;
>   Father and fondler of heart Thou hast wrung:
> Hast thy dark descending and most art merciful then."
>   (G. M. Hopkins, *The Wreck of the Deutschland*)

The psalm has a classical *finale*: a prophetic verdict on those who are the enemies of the psalmist's craving for faith, and a prophetic proclamation of the happiness of the king. (The Hebrew text reads: "The king will be glad in God", etc.; the psalmist here identifies himself with the happiness of the king, who is the representative of the entire people. The present translation replaces this piece of ancient sensibility with a straightforward first person singular.)—"I heard from the throne a loud voice, which said: 'See, this is where God is present among men. He will be in their midst, and they will be his people, and he, God-with-them, will be their God. And he will wipe all tears from their eyes, and there will be no more death nor mourning nor crying nor pain, for the old world is over'" (Apoc. 21. 3-4).

Psalm 69

Save me, God, I am up to my neck in the water,
I am sinking, the mud is sucking me down,
my feet can no longer find firm ground anywhere—
water, only water, the current drags me along.
I am tired with crying, my throat is a burning wound,
my eyes are dead with staring, with waiting for God.

I have more enemies than I have hairs on my head
and I am no match for their hatred and lies.
They demand the return of things which I never stole—
Lord, you would know if I had done any wrong,
for who can hide from you, o powerful God?
No, do not shame those who are waiting for you—
if they see me, what are they to think of you?

Because I have trusted in you they are laughing at me,
yes, I have lost my face and become a stranger,
even my brothers do not recognize me.
My passion for your house has eaten me up,
the names they are calling you are falling on me.
I am crying, I will not eat—they are mocking at it.
I go about in rags—they are saying: that fool!
My name's in the gutter—I feel they are talking about me,
they are making up songs about me in their drunken talk.

Will there be ever an hour of grace for me,
Lord, will your love give an answer, your truth come to save me?
Then pull me up from the mud, or am I to drown
in this contempt, in this abysmal water?
Let the flood, the precipice never devour me,
let the mouth of the grave not close over me.
In your love, God, I would be secure,
as in a mother's womb—after all, I am yours.
Do not turn away, do not be such a silent God,
speak and have mercy upon my anxious soul,
claim me back, set me free from the clutch of my enemies.

You know them by name, all those who rise up against me,
you know how they trample on me, how abased I am.
Shame has broken me down, I am past recovery.
I waited for comfort, but no; I hoped for some one
to bring me relief, but I found no one at all.
They gave me bread—it was bread that had been poisoned,
they gave me drink—I found that it was vinegar.

I wish they would eat till they were ready to burst,
yes, let them choke in their plenty, the whole lot of them.
Strike them with blindness, cripple their loins for ever,
pour out your curses upon them like so many flames,
just let them burn in the blazing fire of your anger.
Turn their city into waste land, drive all life out of it—
when I was beaten by you, they were bold enough then,
when I was wounded by you, they beat me still harder.

Just let them pile up sin upon sin, my God,
and find no grace in your eyes in the hour of your coming.
Lord, wipe out their names from the book of life,
and they will not be recorded among your friends.

But me—you will save me, tormented and poor as I am.
Then I will thank you, sing in praise of your Name—
that will make you happy rather than sacrifices.

The poor and the humble, all who are looking for God,
they may know it, they will come to life in joy.
People in anguish and misery find a hearing—
people in chains, God does not let you down.
Heaven and earth will praise and proclaim his Name,
and also the sea, with all living creatures in it.

He will come to rescue his people, rebuild their cities,
and their children will also live there in peace.
And so his Name will be known and loved, for ever.

[Psalm 69] The psalms are not perfect prayers in the sense that they only express the so-called higher, purer, or more "perfect" emotions. Their perfection lies in their being immersed in the human situation with all its fears, doubts, and crudities, while at the same time bringing God's presence to bear on all this. Chaos, disintegration, injustice, vulgarity, and abuse are real, and as such they can be the stuff of the experience of faith, and in cases even its mainspring. Psalm 69 affords a classical example of the complaint, in which the experience of undeserved suffering is not glossed over but fathomed. A first level of desolation consists in the discovery of loneliness and chaos when friends turn into enemies. But then comes a far worse disillusion: faith in God, no matter how passionate, carries no prestige among these people; on the contrary, it is an occasion for further slights. And it is precisely at this point, when the psalmist realizes that his very faith makes him vulnerable, that he can turn his complaint into a prophetic hymn of thanksgiving, and call upon the poor in spirit and the humble and the whole world to share in his experience.—"Did not the Messiah have to go through all this suffering in order to come to his glory?" (Luke 24. 26).

Psalm 72

Give your wisdom, God, to the king,
lay your kingdom in his hands,
that he may be a shepherd for your people,
for your poor people a righteous judge.
And the mountains will yield sheaves of peace
and the hills will bear a harvest of justice.

He will stand up for the poor and the needy,
do justice to the least of his brothers.
He will break and bind the powers
which are holding us—he will live
and never fail, like the sun,
like the moon, generation after generation.

Like the rain descending on the fields,
like the dew that waters the earth—
thus he will come, and in those days
faithfulness and truth will flourish
and there will be peace in abundance,
until the light of the moon is put out.

He will rule from sea to sea,
from the great River to the end of the earth.
Foreign nations will be forced to stoop,
all his enemies will bite the dust.

Faraway kings, faraway coastlands
come to offer their gifts to him.
Wealthy princes, the richest of lands
lay down their treasures in front of him,
and one day all the great ones on earth
and all nations will kneel before him.

He will be the deliverer of the poor,
a friend to those who have no one.
For humble people he is within reach,
he gives hope to those without rights.
Their blood is precious in his eyes,
he ransoms them from the house of slavery.

And they will live, a golden age,
call him happy day after day,
and pray that it may ever be so:
a flood of wheat, fields that wave,
trees full of fruit, high on the mountains—
a city arises from a sea of green.

His name is in eternity,
as long as the sun is in the heavens.
His name goes round, all over the earth—
a word of peace, from man to man.

[Psalm 72] The idea of royal government in the ancient Near East was so bound up with the risk of idolatry (cf. 1 Sam. 10. 17–19) that Israel was for a long time loath to adopt it. The story of Saul's election and anointing shows Israel's struggle between secularization at the expense of the sole worship of Yahweh, and the desire for national and religious unity after the destruction of the national shrine at Shiloh (1 Sam. 4). When Saul was finally chosen by Samuel he was told that it was the Lord who anointed him and that it was the Lord's people he was going to lead. This conception of the king as "the Lord's Anointed One" was gradually deepened in the course of David's and Solomon's reigns. But when after Solomon's death in 931 B.C. the kingdom fell apart and many of the subsequent kings proved traitors to the God of Israel, Israel's former fears proved to have been only too well grounded. To culminate the disaster, the split kingdom came under continual attacks from the side of Assyria and Babylon. It was then that the prophets began to give expression to Israel's craving for deliverance by projecting the image of the ideal king, who as the Lord's Anointed One (Hebrew: *Mashiah*, Messiah) would bring about God's kingdom. This psalm, attributed by the original text to Solomon, the just and glorious king of peace (*Shelomoh—Shalom*), evokes this eschatological kingdom in the wake of Isaiah (e.g., 11. 1–5) and Zechariah (e.g., 9. 9–10). The oldest Christian traditions have recited this psalm with Jesus Christ in mind, and Matthew's legend of the magi offering their gifts to Jesus must have been inspired by this psalm.

Psalm 73

Yes, surely God
is good for us,
for a man
who has been cleansed.

As for me,
I had almost lost
my foothold, I
had nearly fallen.
I was envious
of that boaster,
I saw his peace
without God.

He has no cares—
excellent health,
no worries about
the sorrows of men,
and never harassed
like everyone else.
Pride is for him
a signet-ring,
craving for power
fits him like a glove.

His eyes are bulging
from his fat face,
his heart brims over
with basest thoughts,
mockery, cynicism,
menace and threats,
and his big mouth
is raised against heaven,
his tongue is spoiling
the whole of the earth.

Of course he carries
the mob with him.
They lap up his words
like so much water—
"What has God
to do with us,
if, that is,
he is still there?"
So he goes his own godless
way with a will.
He is getting on fine
always doing better.

Why did I ever
have faith in you,
why did I keep
my hands clean?
Every day
is punishment to me,
every morning
I am beaten.
I have often thought:
do like those others.
But then I would have
to break with you,
have to deny
the faith of my father.
So I was tossed
backwards and forwards,
harassed, desperate,
without any prospect.

Until I found
peace in your mystery,
and learned to see life
in the light of your future—
the whole of their life
is built on quicksand,
it falls to ruins,
they are in one
fell moment destroyed.
Like an evil dream—
you wipe them out
of the world of men.

I was embittered
and rebellious,
I was hurt
deep in my soul.
I was like a senseless
animal with you.

With you, *Lord,* I am
always with you.
You hold me tight,
your hand in mine.
You will bring all things
to a good end,
you lead me on
in your good pleasure.
What is heaven
to me without you,
where am I on earth
if you are not there?
Though my body
is broken down,
though my heart dies,
You are my Rock,
my God, the future
that waits for me.

Far away from you
life is not life.
To break faith with you
is to be no one.

With you, my highest
good, my God,
with you I am
secure.

[Psalm 73] Psalm 73 is a problem-psalm like Psalms 37 and 49, and in many ways recalls the book of Job. It fathoms in a passionate, and almost rigorous way the power of faith in God by comparing it with unbelief. Rhetorically, the psalm opens with the conclusion: when all is said and told, a man can say that God is good; but he will only be able to say so after he has gone through the experience that faith has not a leg to stand on. Psalm 37 offers the simple solution: the wicked will be destroyed, the just will possess the land. Psalm 49 admits that arrogance is power, but also that it does not last beyond the grave. Both these psalms, however, fail to reach the mystery which lies at the bottom of the problem. In Psalm 73 the fullest possible allowance is made for human prosperity for its own sake, and it is precisely in this way that the poet succeeds in subjecting it to radical criticism: human prestige becomes essentially relative. And his prayer becomes: No matter what happens, You are there. It is this faith that carries him through and beyond all the theories about what will be the lot of power and arrogance. In this way Psalm 73 articulates faith in God as a process of purification, as an inner growth towards communion with God, ultimately in the resurrection.—"Brethren, I may say with all assurance that David, our patriarch, is dead and buried, since we have his tomb among us down to this day. But being a prophet he knew that God had promised him under oath that a descendant of his would sit on his throne. This means that he foresaw and announced the resurrection of Christ, who indeed has not fallen a prey to the Pit, and who has not lived to see corruption. God has raised him up, this Jesus; this is what we bear witness to" (Acts 2. 29–32).

Psalm 80

Shepherd of Israel, hear our prayer.
You, leading Joseph like a flock,
you, enthroned on the winged animals,
guide and blessing of Benjamin,
God of Ephraim and Manasseh,
show your glory for us to see,
stir up your power and come to our rescue.

Be here among us,
light in the midst of us,
be our saviour,
bring us to life.

O Lord, God of the powers, how long yet
will you turn angrily away when we pray?
We have had to eat the bread of tears,
a flood of tears you made us drink.
We are the plaything of our neighbours,
we are the laughing-stock of our enemies.

God of the powers,
light in the midst of us,
be our saviour,
bring us to life.

There was a vine in the land of Egypt,
with tender care you dug it out;
then you drove away other nations
in order to plant it in their land.
You tilled the soil to make it grow,
to let it take root in every place
and spread itself over all the country—
and with its shadow it covers the mountains,
and with its twigs the divine cedars;
it stretches its branches out to the sea,
its tendrils down to the great River.

Why, then, were its fences destroyed?
Why can every passer-by
plunder and loot it, why do the boars
break loose from the forest to trample it down,
why are the vermin stripping it bare?

God of the powers,
be our saviour,
be here among us,
bring us to life.

From your heaven look down on this vine,
go out, recover it, cherish the stock
which you planted with your own hand.
May those who once burnt it like firewood
be consumed in the fire of your anger.
But never again take away your hand,
away from the one whom you have chosen,
away from Man, the son of your mercy.

We will never turn from you again.
Make us new and we call your Name:

God of the powers,
be here among us,
light in the midst of us,
bring us to life.

[Psalm 80] This powerful psalm can be looked upon as the prayerful counterpart of the prophecy addressed to Israel, the Northern kingdom, by Jeremiah's "Book of Comfort" (Jer. 30. 1–31. 22; the references to Judah, the Southern kingdom, are insertions and additions of a later date). Both Jeremiah's "Book of Comfort" and Psalm 80 bear witness to the religious and national revival in Jerusalem under Josiah, king of Judah (640–609 B.C.), who took advantage of the weakness of the Assyrian invaders. He conquered again the lands of the former kingdom of Israel, defeated and deported in 721 B.C., and restored the cult of Yahweh, adulterated for political reasons by a whole series of kings before him. At the heart of this so-called "deuteronomistic" revival (cf. 2 Kings 22. 3–23. 24) was the inspiration of the prophetic movement, which men like Elijah, Elisha, Amos, and Hosea had inaugurated in the North. This was the territory occupied for the most part by the tribes that traced their origin to Jacob's (Jacob = Israel: cf. Gen. 32. 23–31) favourite wife, Rachel: Ephraim and Manasseh, the sons of Joseph (cf. Jer. 31. 15 ff.). There were visions of a restoration of God's own kingdom, which were shattered again when the kingdom of Judah was finally defeated by Nebuchadnezzar in 586 B.C., but which were revived when Cyrus' edict of 538 B.C. allowed the Jews to go back to Jerusalem and rebuild the temple. Thus Psalm 80 has become a passionate appeal to God's faithfulness in terms which recall not only the past glories of the militant theocracy around the Ark, but especially also the prophetic proclamation of Israel's election and rejection, expressed by means of the image of the vine, first used by Hosea (10. 1), and expanded later on, notably in the famous allegories by Isaiah (5. 1–7) and Ezechiel (15. 1–8; 17. 3–10; 19. 10–14).—"I am the true vine, and my Father is the vinedresser. He cuts off every branch of mine that bears no fruit, and he prunes and cleans every branch of mine that does bear fruit, so that it may come to bear more fruit. You are already cleaned thanks to the word which I have spoken to you. Remain in me, as I remain in you" (John 15. 1–4).

79

Psalm 84

I am eaten up with the love of your house,
o God of all the powers.
I am longing heart and soul
for the fore-courts of the Lord,
my whole body is crying and yearning
for the living God.

Every bird will find a home—
even the swallow builds a nest
in the shadow of your altar,
where she may lay down her young
close to you, Lord of all the powers,
to you, my king, my God.

And happy is the man
who may live under your roof—
he will praise you day by day.
Happy are those people,
who will find their strength in you—
your ways are in their hearts.

Are they to pass through a barren valley,
they will make it a valley of springs.
Spring showers will bless the land.
And so they go on as if they had wings,
to find you in your holy city.

Lord of the powers, hear my prayer,
God of Jacob, listen to me:
protect the people whom you have called,
bless us—we are here before you.

One day in your court is better
than a thousand days outside.
And to wait upon the threshold
of the house of our Lord God,
is far better than to waste
away my life in the tents of sin.

The Lord is a sun, the Lord is a shield.
He makes us respected, he makes us loved.
The man who goes on the path of life
upright, without lies, will find
mercy in the eyes of God.

Happy is the man
who will put his trust in you,
o Lord God of all the powers.

[Psalm 84] If Psalm 46 celebrates Yahweh, present on Mount Zion, by enlarging his function as God of the Powers (cf. Ps. 24) to eschatological proportions, this psalm follows a different path: the God of the Armies becomes the God who gives inner safety and reliance, and his Temple is no longer the centre of a military stronghold, but the symbol of the inner strength of the believing community, the faithful "Remnant of Israel", which would survive the disillusions of the captivity thanks to a deepened sense of faith. In this way Psalm 84 also reflects the mood of the period of the Second Temple, built between 520 and 515 B.C., which became the spiritual home, not only of the Jews that had come back to Jerusalem, but also of those many Jews who in the course of the centuries of disintegration had settled elsewhere, for example, in Egypt or Babylon, and become the pilgrim Jews regularly going up to Jerusalem. Psalm 84 can therefore be looked upon, together with Psalms 42–43, as the background of the collection of the "Songs of Ascents" (Pss. 120–134).—"No one can be the servant of two masters, for he will either dislike the one and love the other, or be devoted to the one and despise the other. You cannot be the servants of God and of Vested Interest. That is why I am telling you: do not worry about your lives, about what you will eat or drink or put on. Is not life more than food, and is not the body more than clothes? Look at the birds in the sky: they neither sow nor reap nor store up food, and yet your heavenly Father feeds them" (Matt. 6. 24–26).

Psalm 85

Again and again you have favoured your land,
o God, and changed our lives for the better.
You have covered all our sins,
taken away all guilt from your people,
again and again revoked your threats
and quenched the burning fire of your anger.

Now be merciful to us again
and no longer embittered, or would you be angry
for ever with us, throughout all generations?
Would you not rather see us alive
so that we may be glad in you?
Give us a sign of your covenant, then,
God of love, restore us to honour.

I want to hear the word of the Lord.
Peace—that is the word of the Lord.
For his people, for his followers,
for whoever turns back to him,
the Lord holds out a word of peace.
Yes, his rescue is close for them,
his glory will be at home in their land.

Mercy and faithful love will meet,
truth and peace will embrace one another.
Faithfulness sprouts like a seed in the earth,
truth is like a sun in the sky.
Our Lord God will lavish blessing,
and the land will bear its fruit.
Truth, like a messenger, runs on ahead of him,
peace follows him wherever he goes.

[Psalm 85] Psalm 85 is a prayer for a second Exodus experience: the People comes back from exile, and God returns to the Land of Jacob—the Hebrew word for "turn round", "come back" occurs no less than five times in the original. Its scene, like that of Psalm 84, is the return to Jerusalem after the great captivity and the building of the Second Temple. Its spiritual background is formed by the famous "Book of Israel's Comfort" by the anonymous author of Isaiah 40–55 and by the prophecies of Zechariah 1–8, both of which date from the same period. Its characteristic attitudes are those which gradually developed through the activities of the prophets: dispositions of the heart have become the basis of the experience of God's "glory" in the midst of the community rather than national and ritual assurances.—"The fruit of the Spirit is: love, joy, patience, kindness, goodness, faithfulness and mutual trust, gentleness and recollection—no law can touch people who are such. Those who belong to Jesus, the Christ, have crucified their selfish nature with its passions and desires. If we live by the Spirit, let us then also act according to the Spirit" (Gal. 5. 22–25).

Psalm 90

You have been a safe place to live in,
for us, o Lord, throughout all generations.
Even before the mountains were born
and the whole of this world was brought forth,
within living memory you are God,
and in all ages to come.

You make people crumble into dust,
you say: it's all over, ah children of Adam.
In your sight, a thousand years
are like yesterday, a day that has passed,
are like an hour of watching by night.
You sweep us out like a dream in the morning,
we are like the vigorous grass that grows—
it comes up at daybreak and flourishes,
at dusk it is mown down and dead.

Yes, we are perishing with your rage,
eaten up with anxiety when you are angry.
For you remember all our sins,
our innermost secrets are before your eyes—
that is why our days are so trivial,
our years as fleeting as a sigh.

The life of a man lasts seventy years,
or eighty, if we are strong.
Most of that is hardship and sorrow—
all at once it is over and we are gone.
Who can fathom the power of your rage,
and who is aware how fearful you are?
Teach us, then, so to value our days
that we may learn to cherish wisdom.

How long must we still wait for you?
O God, come back, and make peace with us.
Do not hold back your grace any longer
and we will from now on be glad in you.
And give us as many happy days
as we have suffered days of misery.

Show us that you are at work for us,
and let our children see your glory.
Be all around us with your mildness,
o Lord, and let the work of our hands be lasting,
let the work of our hands be lasting.

[Psalm 90] This psalm, which the Hebrew Bible calls "The Prayer of Moses, the Man of God", is a meditation on the question: What is Man? The poem is entirely in the vein of the wisdom-tradition, one of the classical elements in the Bible, although its incorporation into it is of a relatively late date. Besides the Law with its many cultic prescriptions and the inspired word of hope and fear, the utterances of the priests and the prophets respectively, there had always been a kind of culture of human wisdom in Israel as well as in the Ancient Near East as a whole. This experience found expression, not so much in formalized philosophy as in endless collections of *meshalim*, short, pithy proverbs and sayings, which could be expanded into parables, allegories, symbolic fables, and suchlike. Its practitioners were the "wise men" (cf. Jer. 8. 9–10; 18. 18). And just as Moses and Aaron passed for the prophet and priest *par excellence*, and David was considered the original mind behind the psalms, so the schools of wise men liked to point to Solomon as to their prime example, and even attributed their collected sayings to him (cf. Prov. 1. 1; 25. 1; 1 Kings 4. 29–34). But Jewish wisdom always distinguished itself from the wisdom of its neighbours by its being related to the awe of Israel's God. True human wisdom is only achieved by putting it to the test of God's eternal and inscrutable wisdom, shown in Creation and in the Law. Psalm 90 is a fine example of this "ecstatic humanism", and was composed on the basis of the same experiences that went into the making of the stories of the Fall and the Deluge (Gen. 3; 6) and the Book of Job. The experience of the contrast between human frailty and God's eternal reliability is deepened to an awareness of the contrast between sinfulness and holiness, and then turned into a prayer for "wisdom"— the ability to feel strengthened by God's faithfulness, even to the point of death.—"God has chosen what is foolish in the eyes of the world to put the wise to shame; God has chosen what is weak in the eyes of the world to put the strong to shame; God has chosen what is of low birth and insignificant; he has chosen what is nothing, in order to bring to nothingness what is something. Thus no human being can afford to boast in the presence of God. It is thanks to him that you are now alive in Jesus, the Christ, who on God's behalf has become all our wisdom" (1 Cor. 1. 27–30).

Psalm 91

Whoever lives in the shelter of the most high God
and spends the night in the shadow of God almighty—
he says to the Lord: my refuge, my stronghold,
my God, in you I put all my trust.

He sets you free from the nets of the bird-catcher,
he keeps the plague of evil from you,
he will cover you with his feathers,
under his wings you will find safety.

In the dead of night you have nothing to fear;
neither dread in the daytime a stab in the back,
nor fear the plague that stalks in the darkness—
no fever will ruin you in the heat of day.

Although a thousand fall at your side,
ten thousand go down before your eyes,
it will not touch you, your God is faithful,
he is a shield, a wall round about you.

You have only to lift up your eyes
to see how wickedness is avenged.
Then you say: "The Most High is my refuge",
and you will be at home with him.

No disasters will happen to you,
no pestilence will come close to your tent.
He has sent his angels out,
to guard you at every step you take.

They will bear you up on their hands—
no stone will hurt your feet on your way.
You plant your foot on the head of the lion,
you will trample on the snake, you will kill the dragon.

"Yes, if he clings to me I will rescue him,
I will make him great, for he holds on to my Name.
If he calls, I will answer. In anguish and need: I with him,
I will make him free and clothe him with glory.

He shall live to be full of years.
He shall live to see my rescue."

[Psalm 91] This impressive psalm shows how the different traditions of Old Testament religious experience were fused when the priestly class and the schools of wise men in Jerusalem set about collecting, editing, commenting on, and adding to, the existing oral and written literary deposits of Israel at the time of the Second Temple. The psalm opens with four traditional divine names. *Elyon* (Most High God) is originally a name derived from the Phoenician pantheon and used for the deity at the Canaanite sanctuary at Jerusalem (cf. Gen. 14. 17–19). *El Shadday* (Almighty God, or perhaps: God of the Mountains) is the ancient divine name going back to the days of the patriarchs (cf. Gen. 17, 1). *Yahweh* (in reading the Bible aloud always substituted by *Adonay*, Lord) was used mostly in the tradition of the Southern kingdom of Judah, whereas *Elohim* (God) was used mostly in the Northern kingdom of Israel. The spirituality of Psalm 91 harks back to the desert experience of the Exodus, which under the influence of the prophetic and wisdom traditions is presented as the model of the life of every believer. Priestly influence is noticeable in the cultic setting of the psalm: a liturgical proclamation of the assurance with which the man who believes can make his way through life, clinched by a divine oracle to confirm the proclamation. The oldest layers of the Christian tradition have presented Jesus as fulfilling this psalm: the strongly symbolic accounts of Jesus' Baptism and Temptations have been composed with, among other things, this psalm in mind (cf. Matt. 3. 16; 4, 6. 11). And in the wake of Jesus the messengers of the kingdom will lead their lives strengthened by the same assurance (cf. Luke 10. 18).—"Let us not put the Lord to the test, as some of them did, only to be destroyed by the serpents. Do not grumble as some of them did, only to be destroyed by the Destroyer. What happened to them is a warning to us, and it was recorded for our instruction, since we are the witnesses of the fulfilment of time. Let therefore everyone who thinks that he stands take care not to fall. You are not exposed to any temptation that exceeds your human limits. And God is faithful: he will not let you be put to the test above your strength. With the temptation he provides the way out of it, so that you may endure it" (1 Cor. 10. 9-13).

Psalm 93

The Lord our God is king,
majesty is his robe,
strength he wears for a garment.

Unshakeable is the earth,
unshakeably firm is your throne,
you are from everlasting.

The seas are raising, o Lord,
the seas are raising their voices,
their floods of thundering breakers.

More powerful than the voice of that water,
more powerful than the waves of the sea,
are you, the God of the heavens.

Your word is unfailing and faithful,
may your house be holy,
Lord God, for ever and ever.

[Psalm 93] Psalms 93–100, the so-called "royal psalms", form, like Psalms 46–48, a collection of hymns celebrating God's presence in the Temple. There he manifests himself to the cultic community, not only as the giver of the faith-inspiring word of the law, but also as the king of the awe-inspiring order of the world (cf. Ps. 19). It was in the atmosphere of common worship in the Temple that the *kebod Jahweh*, the Glory of the Lord, was evoked and revealed: Psalm 150 provides an eloquent inventory of liturgical expedients used to express and actualize the common faith. And the content of the experience was: God is present among us, he will make his word come true, he will also be faithful to his own creation. The latter conviction is amply elaborated in psalms like 104; Psalm 93 only expresses the experience of God's presence: "The Lord of the earth has shown himself" (Ps. 114).—"Jesus woke up and rebuked the wind, and said to the sea: 'Silence! Be quiet!' And the wind ceased, and a great calm ensued. He said to them: 'Why are you afraid? Have you no faith?' And they became full of awe, and said to each other: 'Who is then this man, that even the wind and the sea obey him?'" (Mark 4. 39–41).

Psalm 95

We must sing at the top of our voices,
rejoice before God, the rock of our safety,
appear before him, giving thanks and playing,
and shout: "He is a powerful God,
a king far greater than all the gods."

The depths of the earth belong to him,
the highest mountains, they are his.
The sea is his, it is he who made it,
the land was modelled by his hands.

Come and bow before him in worship,
kneel to the God who created us all.
He is our God, he is our Shepherd,
and we are the people, the flock of his hand.

II

Listen, then, to his voice to-day:

"Do not become hard, as once you did
in that place of discord, that day of your Testing,
when your fathers defied me in the desert,
and yet they had seen what I had done.
For forty years I loathed that generation.
I said: that people with their hearts gone astray,
they neither know nor want my ways.
So, in my anger, I took an oath—
never will they come into my Rest."

[Psalm 95] This psalm, a dramatic liturgical invitation to worship followed by a prophetic oracle, has for centuries been sung as the *invitatorium*, the beginning of the daily Office in the Latin Church. It is again an exploration into the divine names—God, King, Rock, Shepherd, *Yahweh*. The last of these names, rendered here by "he" and "him" at the example of Martin Buber's translation, is the key to understanding Israel's attitude towards God. When according to the tradition of Exodus 3. 13–15 Moses heard the ineffable Name in the desert, it was after a common literary convention explained by popular etymology, and taken to mean: "I am who I am". Translated into modern idiom this Hebrew locution would run: "I am with you, so do not ask any questions". For all his closeness, the God of Israel remains infinitely transcendent, and for all his transcendence, he remains infinitely close. Thus he is the faithful and gracious Shepherd of Psalm 23, but also the King of Glory of Psalms 24 and 93. Thus he is the "ground of being, and granite of it" (G. M. Hopkins), the Rock of salvation and safety, from which the water flowed when Israel was at a loss in the desert. It is from this last point that the prophetic warning of the second part of the psalm takes its start. It was in the desert, near Kadesh, the "holy place", or—according to a different tradition—near Sinai, the mountain that was looked upon as the prototype of the later Temple (cf. Exod. 25. 40), that the faith of the People of God did not stand up to the test: they in their turn tested Yahweh's reliability by defying him, so that the names of that place became known as *Meribah* (discord) and *Massah* (test) (cf. Num. 20. 1–13; Exod. 17. 1–7).—"Everyone who hears these words of mine and acts upon them will be like a wise man who built his house on the rock. And the rain fell, and the floods came, and the winds blew and threw themselves upon that house, but it did not collapse because it had been founded on the rock" (Matt. 7. 24–25).

Psalm 97

The Lord our God is king,
all the shores on earth
are laughing and shouting for joy.
He lives in clouds and darkness,
righteousness and truth
support his royal throne.

Fire sweeps on before him,
it burns his enemies away.
It flashes across the earth.
The whole of the world has seen it.
The earth was writhing and groaning
like a woman in labour.

Mountains melt like wax
wherever our God appears,
lord and master on earth.
The heavens have proclaimed,
the pagans have come to see
his love in all its splendour.

Shame upon the man
who bows down before statues,
who prides himself on nothing.
Must not all the gods
bow to the ground before him,
kneel down before our God?

Zion has heard it, the cities
of Judah shout for joy
because you are their saviour.
O Lord, most high God,
you are much more, much greater
than all the gods of the earth.

All those who hate what is evil
are loved by the Lord our God;

he has their hearts in his keeping.
And he will one day
set all his loved ones free
from the grasp of evil for ever.

Light is sown like seed
for God's own righteous friends,
gladness will be flourishing.
Friends, rejoice, be glad,
and proclaim his Name
high above all names.

[Psalm 97] This hymn is a patchwork composition of many standard idioms from the book of psalms. It first expresses the experience of God's presence in a series of cosmic images, and then goes
on to face the believing community with a final option: they will
either be subject to the powers of the world and live according to
their norms, or they will experience the joy of relying on the king
of all the gods of the earth. This fundamental connection between
God's kingship and the simple justice of God's friends is also the
subject of a passage in Isaiah, which in many ways is comparable to
Psalm 96: the first of the four so-called "Songs of the Servant of
Yahweh" (Is.42. 1–9; the other three: 49. 1–6; 50. 4–11; 52. 13–53.
12, cf. Ps. 22). The poet of this Song, however, puts rather more
emphasis on the unobtrusive righteousness of the mysterious servant of Yahweh by first presenting him as the manifestation of God's
goodness, which is then celebrated as God's royal victory afterwards.—"Jesus withdrew, but there were many who followed him.
He healed them all, but also told them not to make him known.
Thus the word of the prophet Isaiah was fulfilled: 'Behold, my
servant, whom I have chosen, my beloved one, the man of all my
favour. I will make my Spirit rest upon him, and he will bring the
message of true faith in God to the nations. He will not quarrel or
shout, and his voice will not be heard in the streets. He will not
break a bruised reed or quench a smouldering wick before he has
led the true faith in God to its triumph—all the nations will put
their trust in his name'" (Matt. 12. 15–21; cf. Is. 42. 1–4).

Psalm 103

I want to call him by his Name,
the holy God, as truly as I live.
I thank him from the bottom of my heart,
and I will forget none of his benefits.

He is the forgiveness of my sins,
he will heal me, time after time.
He calls my life away from the grave,
surrounds me with goodness and tender love.
He fills my days with happiness,
and like an eagle my youth revives.

He makes good whatever he has promised,
he takes the part of all the oppressed.
He made known his Name to Moses,
and all the people saw his works—
merciful Lord, God full of grace,

faithful, endlessly patient love.
He does not quarrel with us to the end,
he does not haunt us with our sins,
he will not repay evil with evil,
he is greater than our sins.

Yes, what the heavens are for the earth,
that is his love for those who believe.
As far as the east is away from the west,
so far away from us he throws our sins.
Just as a man is merciful to his sons,
so is he a merciful father to us,
because he knows us—he has not forgotten
that we are made of the dust of the earth.

People—their days are like the grass,
they bloom like flowers in the open field;

then the wind blows, and they are gone
and no one can tell where they once stood.
Only the love of God will be lasting,
and age after age he will do justice
to all who hold on to his covenant,
who take his word to heart and fulfil it.

He is king, his throne is the heavens,
he is powerful all over the earth.
Bless him, then, you angels of God,
strong men, carrying out his word.
Powers and authorities, you must praise him,
faithful servants, who do his will.
Bless him, all you works of God,
all over the world—he is your king.

I want to call him by his Name,
the holy God, as truly as I live.

[Psalm 103] This psalm, a confession of divine forgiveness and patience supporting and guiding human frailty and sinfulness, shows very well how Israel could be creative in lending fresh vigour to the old, rugged traditions about her own origin. The evocation of the presence of a God who is merciful rather than unflinchingly just, and whose reliability extends beyond the grave, is firmly referred to Exodus 33–34. After the breach of the Covenant around the golden calf and Moses' dramatic intercession (Exod. 32), God continues the journey with Israel: he passes before Moses, exclaiming his Name and professing his mercy (Exod. 34. 4–9), renews the Covenant and gives the Law. This is how God deals with frail and sinful people; their sins are no obstacle to his abiding presence. This basic conviction, the core of the Exodus message, is here orchestrated by means of a subtle chain of images and metaphors, which actualize and give new depth to the old story of human sin and divine rescue. And so this very poetical expression of faith finally returns to a new recognition of God's kingship, now no longer a reason to cower, but a challenge to be confident and face the future.—"Children, let our love not consist in thoughts or words, but in acts and in truth. By this we will know that we are the children of truth, and then we may also reassure our own hearts in God's presence whenever our hearts accuse us. For God is greater than our hearts, and he knows everything" (1 John 3. 18–20).

Psalm 104

I want to call you, God, by your Name,
as truly as I live.

My Lord and my God, you are great and tremendous,
clothed with splendour and majesty,
and with a mantle of light wrapped around you.
You stretch out the heavens like a tent,
you build your lofty halls on the water,
you ride the clouds, they are your chariot,
and high up on the wings of the wind
you make your way, and the storm is your messenger,
burning fires, they are your servants.
You have firmly founded the earth,
in eternity it will not be shaken;
the sea once covered it like a cloak,
the water was still above the mountains—
then it took to flight when you threatened it,
it was gone at the voice of your thunder.
The mountains stand up, the valleys spread out,
and all things find the place you intended.
You have set limits to the flood,
never again will it conquer the earth.

You make the springs well up in the valleys,
and the streams are flowing between the mountains.
They water all the beasts of the field,
the wild ass quenches his thirst from them.
There the birds of the sky are living,
high among the branches they sing their songs.
The mountains are watered by the clouds,

the whole earth drinks its fill from your rain.
You just let the grass grow for the cattle,
and green crops for man to look after.
And so he produces corn from the earth,
and harvests the wine that makes his heart glad,
and also the oil that makes his skin glisten,
and the bread too that keeps him alive.
God's own trees are in full flower,
the cedars of Lebanon, which he has planted.
The birds have begun their nests in them,
high up in the tops the storks have their homes.
The high mountains are for the wild goats,
badgers take shelter among the rocks.

You are the creator of moon and time,
you, the creator of sun and of sunset.
You darken the world—at once it is night,
and the whole of the forest begins to stir:
the young lions are roaring for prey,
they are asking God for their food.
The sun rises and they slink back,
and in their dens they lie down again.
Now man goes out to do his work,
he labours until darkness falls.
And all this, God, is your own work—
your wisdom speaks from so many things,
your power of creation fills our earth.

And then the sea, so wide and enormous,
teeming with animals, great and small—
there the ships sail to and fro,

there is Leviathan, the monster,
made by you, for you to play with.

Everything waits for you full of hope,
all the living ask you for food.
You give it to them, always in time,
you open your hand and they eat their fill.
If you turn away they are frightened,
if you take their breath they die,
and they fall back into the dust.
But send your spirit, and they come to life,
you give the earth the freshness of youth.

Thus the world is full of him,
glory to God and lasting joy.

If he looks at the earth it trembles,
if he touches the mountains they burn.
As long as I am I will sing to him,
a song to my God while I am alive.
I hope that this song will make him happy,
I am happy myself with you, my God.
And let there be upon earth an end
to all evil, to every sin.

I want to call you, God, by your Name,
as truly as I live.

[Psalm 104] Israel experienced the glory and the faithful love of her God in the rescue from Egypt and the introduction, by Covenant and Promise, into Canaan. As Israel's faith was widened and deepened, she came to realize that the God of her rescue was also the God who made the world. The first chapter of Genesis was composed to bear witness to this faithful realization, and Psalm 104, which has its parallels in other literatures of the Ancient Near East, orchestrates this even more abundantly: the man who has the eyes of faith can interpret the marvels of creation as manifestations of God's glory and reliability. "From the creation of the world his invisible being has been perceived by human reason in his works" (Rom. 1. 20). The conclusion of this psalm is therefore the same as that of the psalms that deal with Israel's salvation: the People of God have to be faithful to the Word of God, of which it is the depositary.—It is from this concrete, lyrical and in a way very "secular" prayer that the Christian tradition has taken one of its strongest liturgical formulas to express its belief in the life-giving power of God's holy Spirit.

Psalm 105

Proclaim the Name of the Lord,
proclaim his wonderful acts.
Let it be known to the world
that he does wonders for us.
Let all who look for him
be glad with all their hearts—
for who would fail to glory
in his holy Name?
Turn to him, he is powerful,
do not give up looking for him.
Remember, then, his promise,
the signs he gave to us,
you, sons of his servant Abraham,
you, sons of Jacob, his friend.
He is our God, he alone,
his wisdom fills the whole earth.
He always remembers his covenant,
for a thousand generations—
that word which he gave to Abraham,
that oath which he swore to Isaac,
renewed and sealed before Jacob,
a covenant forever with his people—
"I will give you Canaan,
there you will live for good."

They were just a handful of people,
a little group of strangers,
homeless, in the midst of pagans,
wanderers, now here, now there.
But he allowed no one
to tyrannize over them,
he even punished kings
for their sake, and he said:

"Do not touch my anointed,
do no harm to my prophets."

Famine struck the country,
and they ran out of all bread.
Then he sent a man ahead of them,
Joseph, sold as a slave,
accused and thrown into prison—
his feet were painfully fettered
and chains put around his neck—
until he interpreted dreams
and what he foretold came true.
Then the king gave him his freedom,
the Pharao of the Egyptians,
and put everything in his hands,
his house and all his possessions—
he became the adviser of wise men,
the court was subject to him.

And Israel went into Egypt,
Jacob was a welcome guest,
there, in the land of Ham.
There the Lord made them fertile,
more numerous than the Egyptians,
and that annoyed the Egyptians,
they began to hate Israel,
they dared to torment Israel,
with violence and with cunning.
But the Lord called Moses, his servant,
and chose his brother Aaron—
he made them accomplish wonders
there, in the land of Ham.
And he sent darkness down,
it became as dark as the earth,
water was changed into blood,

and all the fish were killed.
The country was swarming with frogs—
they overran the king's palace.
He spoke, and there were the gnats,
mosquitoes throughout their country.
Hail and fire rained down—
the figtree and the vine
lay stretched out on the ground
and all the trees were shattered
everywhere round about.
He spoke, and there were the locusts,
swarms of teeming vermin—
not a blade of grass was left,
they stripped the country bare.
Then he struck their first-born,
the first-fruits of their strength.
Then he led his people to freedom:
there were the tribes, setting out,
loaded with silver and gold,
and nobody tried to harm them.
Egypt, crippled with terror,
Egypt was glad that they went.

He sent a cloud along
to cover them in the rear,
and a fire to give light in the dark.
They asked him: "Give us food"—
and he made quails come down.
He gave them bread from heaven,
and they were no longer hungry.
He tore the rocks apart,
and there was water gushing out,
streams of living water
in the very heart of the desert.
And he did all these things

because he had once made a promise
to Abraham, his servant.

He gave his people freedom,
and shouting for joy we went out.
He gave us the lands of the pagans,
he gave us the works of their hands,
so that we might keep his words,
and live in the light of his covenant,
and praise and give thanks to him,
now and for ever and ever.

[Psalm 105] The body of this "catechetical" psalm recites again
the old story of Israel's rescue from Egypt, the creed which the Jews
have never tired of telling down to our own day (cf., e.g., Deut. 6.
20–25; 26. 5–10): a handful of straying nomads, "wandering
Arameans", made into a people, brought to Egypt and rescued
from it again. But the story in itself is not the only, nor perhaps
even the main, concern of the psalm: the story is bracketed by
references to the "Promise". Israel has to "remember" that her
God was as good as his word, and thus the remembrance, the
anamnesis, becomes a pledge of God's continuing reliability.—
This is also the message of this psalm "to all who imitate the faith
of the father of us all, Abraham. Of him it is written: 'I have made
you the father of many peoples.' And this he is in the sight of God,
in whom he believed, who makes the dead come to life and calls
into existence what does not exist. Hoping against all hope he
believed (. . .). And these words were written down, not only for his
sake, but also for our sake (. . .) since we believe in him who has
raised Jesus, who is our Lord, from the dead" (Rom. 4. 16–18,
23–24).

Psalm 110

Word of God
to my king and lord:
"Take your seat
at my right hand.
I make your enemy
the step of your throne.
I put in your hand
the sceptre of my power.
Rule from Zion
over your enemy.
You are king
on the day of your birth,
light from light,
I have begotten you—
dew from the womb
of the break of day."

Word of God,
inviolable oath:
"You are a priest
in eternity,
just as once
Melchizedek was."

He is your God,
he is at your side.
When the day
of his anger has come
you will crush
the heads of kings;
you summon nations
to come to judgment,

heads are falling
throughout the land.
You drink from the brook,
and, victorious,
you go your way,
head held high.

[Psalm 110] The literary form of this psalm is a congratulation
addressed to the king on the day of his accession to the throne.
The king of Israel is the personification of the people as a whole, and
as such he is God's chosen one *par excellence*, the priestly mediator
of his people with God, and God's agent in bringing about his
kingdom.—The oldest layers of the Christian tradition, following
Jewish traditions about the Messiah, have already used this psalm
to articulate the Christian faith in Christ's pre-eminence: cf. Mark
12. 35–37; Heb. 1. 13; 5. 6; 7. 17, 21; 10. 13.—"We give thanks to
the Father, for he has enabled us to have a share in the inheritance
of the saints in the light. He has rescued us from the powers of darkness and transferred us to the kingdom of his beloved Son" (Col.
1. 12–13).

Psalm 114

When Israel came away from Egypt,
the children of Jacob,
away from a strange and gabbling people,
then the Lord made
of Judah his holy dwelling-place,
his kingdom of Israel.
When the sea saw it, it took to flight,
and the Jordan shrank back,
the mountains and hills, like rams, like sheep,
like lambs, they were jumping.
Sea, what is wrong, that you take to flight?
Why creep away, Jordan?
And mountains, why like rams, like lambs,
why are you jumping?

The Lord of the earth has shown himself,
the God of Jacob,
who changes rocks into springs and pools,
stones into water.

[Psalm 114] An old popular hymn to celebrate the dramatic experience of Israel's election to be God's own people. The rescue from Egypt is described in terms that bear out Israel's triumphant disdain of the pagans. But also the elements of Nature are held up to ridicule by the people of the Covenant: it marches through the water—symbol of chaos—of the Red Sea (Exod. 14) and—according to a different tradition of the Exodus story—the Jordan (Jos. 3); the mountains—the traditional habitats of local deities—are startled like a flock of sheep. Thus Israel again expresses its faith in a God who can save men ("God of Jacob") because he is greater than the powers of the world ("God of the earth").—"I tell you, if your faith is like a mustard-seed, you will say to this mountain: 'Move from here to there'" (Matt. 17. 20).

Psalm 115

Not to us is the honour due, God, not to us,
but to you alone.
For you are reliable mercy and love,
God here among us.

How, then, can there be people who ask:
"Where is that God of yours?"
Our God is above everything,
what he wants he makes.

Pagans make their gods for themselves,
out of silver and gold;
they have mouths, but they cannot speak,
eyes, and they cannot see;
they have ears, but they cannot hear,
and noses, but they cannot smell;
and their hands—they do not feel,
and their feet—they do not walk,
and from their throats, and from their throats
no sound will ever come.
And the man who relies on gods of that kind
is quite as worthless as they are.

Israel, keep on trusting your God,
he is your help and your shield.
All of you, who in the house of God
perform your services, continue to trust him,
he is your help and your shield.
People of God, always keep trusting,
he is your help and your shield.

The Lord God keeps us in his heart
and gives us his blessing.
Happiness and blessing for Israel,

and much happiness for all who serve him,
nothing but mercy for all his people,
great and small.

He will make us great and numerous,
and also our children.
We are the favourites of God,
he has created heaven and earth.
The heaven is the Lord's own heaven,
he has given the earth to men.

Not the dead will speak of him,
not the dead in their dead silence.
But living men—we make him happy,
now and for ever.
Halleluiah.

[Psalm 115] Ever since the first important Greek version of the Old Testament, the so-called Septuagint, was made a few centuries B.C., there has been a tradition to consider this psalm as forming a unity with Psalm 114. The memory of Israel's rescue from Egypt does indeed act as the basis on which this liturgical psalm encourages the whole people, Israelites, priests, and non-Jewish worshippers, to go on relying on their God, who is still with them. The mockery of the idols, which reminds of the famous satire in Isaiah 44. 9–20, is used to strengthen this trust, and the psalm ends with the assurance that Man is not subject to the powers of this world: "He has given the earth to men" (cf. also 1 John 5. 4)—"In all these things we are more than victorious through him who has loved us. For I am sure that neither death nor life, neither angels nor authorities, neither the present nor the future, neither powers nor height nor depth nor any other creature will be able to separate us from the faithful love of God, which is present in Christ Jesus, our Lord" (Rom. 8. 38–39).

Psalm 118

Give thanks to God, for he is good,
his love endures in eternity.
All of Israel must proclaim:
his love endures in eternity—
and all the priests in the house of God:
his love endures in eternity—
all who put their faith in our God:
his love endures in eternity.

I was imprisoned, I called:
"God"—and he gave me an answer,
he gave great freedom to me.

He stands up for me, I am safe,
who will be able to touch me?
He stands up for me like a friend,
and my enemies count for nothing.
Better to shelter with God
than to rely on people;
better to shelter with God
than to rely on power.

All nations surrounded me,
I beat them down with the Name of God.
They closed in on me from every side,

I beat them down with the name of God.
They set upon me like a swarm of wasps,
a buzzing straw-fire round about me,
I beat them down with the Name of God.

I was beaten, I had fallen,
God has helped me to my feet.
He is my pride, he is my song,
my God has become my victory.

Shouts of gladness and triumph are
ringing out from the tents of the righteous:
"The powerful hand of the Lord does wonders,
raised up high, ready to bless us,
the powerful hand of the Lord does wonders."

I shall not die, no, I shall live,
bear witness to his powerful works—
it is true, the Lord has beaten me hard,
but he did not give me up to death.

Open to me
the door of his house,
I want to enter,
I want to thank him.

This door opens
the way to God;
men of good will
may go inside.

I give you thanks, for you have heard me,
you have become my victory.
The stone the builders could not use
has become the cornerstone.
This way God has let it happen—
we see, but fail to understand.
This is the day which the Lord has made,
a day of gladness for all of us.
Come and save us, you, our God,
bring us to a happy end.

You are blessed if you come in the Name of the Lord.
From his house we wish you blessing.
His light has risen over us.
Form a festive procession, then,
and come close around the altar,
wave palm-branches and sing to him:
You are my God, I want to thank you,
my God, and praise you to the skies.

Give thanks to God, for he is good,
his love endures in eternity.

[Psalm 118] A hymn of thanksgiving in the form of an elaborate liturgy at the gates of the Temple. After an introductory hymn that repeats the standard ritual chorus in praise of God's Covenant, an important person, perhaps the king, recounts his rescue from distress, enlarging it to national proportions and thus referring his personal salvation to the salvation of Israel as a people. After a dialogue at the gates of the Temple comes the thanksgiving proper, followed by acclamations, a blessing pronounced by the priests, and an invitation to a ritual procession. The psalm closes with a repetition of the chorus of praise. This liturgical setting is at least partly also a literary convention, as is suggested by the very general terms of the account of the distress and the rescue from it. In this way the psalm has come to acquire a much more general significance.—The Christian tradition spontaneously interpreted this psalm as an Easter hymn. The stone rejected by the builders is one of the oldest images for Jesus (cf., e.g., Mark 12. 10–11; 1 Peter 2. 7), who was received into Jerusalem by the crowd using the blessing taken from this psalm (cf. Mark 11. 9–10).—"In the days of his mortal life Jesus prayed with loud cries and with tears, imploring God, who could save him from death. He was heard on account of his righteousness: although he was Son of God, he learned obedience through suffering, and thus God brought him to perfect glory" (Heb. 5. 7–9).

Psalm 121

I raise my eyes up to the mountains—
will anyone come to help me?
Yes, my God comes to help me,
the maker of heaven and earth.

He will not allow you to stumble,
he will not sleep, he keeps watch over you.
No, he will not slumber or sleep,
he watches over all of his people.

Our God is keeping watch,
like a shadow spread over you.
The sun will not strike you by day,
and by night the moon will not harm you.

He keeps all evil away,
he takes you under his care.
And whether you are coming or going,
God will keep you for ever.

[Psalm 121] Each of the Psalms 120–134 bears the title: "Song of Ascents", in the original. They are all hymns used by pilgrims "going up" to the Temple in Jerusalem, the house of God, "the Maker of Heaven and Earth". Psalm 121 has the literary form of a dialogue between the pilgrim and the priest. Instead of looking for help to the mountains, the traditional places of idolatrous worship, the pilgrim puts his trust in the Creator. The priest confirms his trust by proclaiming that the Maker of heaven and earth is also the God who keeps people on their ways and who cares for their personal well-being. The pilgrimage, of course, is the image for the life of the believer: ever since Abraham felt the call to leave his certainties behind (cf. Gen. 12. 1), this has been one of the most telling images of the Jewish and Christian traditions.—"We do not have a lasting city here, but seek the city that is to come" (Heb. 13. 14).

Psalm 122

It was a joy for me to hear:
"We are on our way to the house of the Lord."
And now we are here in front of your gates,
on your ground, Jerusalem.

City of my heart, Jerusalem,
with your houses shoulder to shoulder.
All the tribes of Israel
are going there, caravans of people,

to celebrate the Name of the Lord,
for this is our sacred duty.
There the seats of judgment are,
there is the royal throne of David.

Pray for peace, for peace on this city,
wish its children every blessing—
city of peace, within your walls
a man may be safely happy.

I wish you all prosperity,
dearest home of all my friends,
city of God, I wish you peace,
peace for evermore.

[Psalm 122] The pilgrims have arrived in Jerusalem: they burst out into a hymn of praise and prayer. The Hebrew text exploits the name *Yerushalayim*, as in some other psalms, for a number of significant word-plays: sh*a'alu*, (pray), sh*alom* (peace), *yi*shl*ayu* (have rest), sh*alwah* (happiness); these strongly emotional over-tones have been made explicit in the translation.—"According to God's promise we expect a new heaven and a new earth, where justice will prevail" (2 Peter 3. 14). "And I saw a new heaven and a new earth. The first heaven and the first earth were vanished and there was no sea any more. And I saw the holy city, Jerusalem, coming down from the heavens, from God" (Apoc. 21. 1–2).

Psalm 123

I raise up my eyes to you,
my God, to you in heaven.

Just as the eyes of a servant will
turn to the hand of his master,
just as the eyes of a slave-girl will
turn to the hand of her mistress,
so our eyes turn to the Lord our God,
until he will show mercy.

Have mercy, Lord, have mercy on us,
God, we are tired of this contempt.

We are sick and tired to death
with the way they have trampled on us and scorned us,
in their recklessness,
in their self-conceit.

[Psalm 123] It took centuries before Israel learned how to pray with a naked faith like this. For centuries there had been visible blessings as signs of God's mercy: the rescue from Egypt, the successful tribal settlements in Canaan, the political power of David's kingdom. As Israel was gradually stripped from these and became a dispersed people, the problem of the happiness of power and arrogance became an ever more pressing challenge to faith, and even the restored community in Jerusalem immediately after the great captivity and in Nehemiah's days saw many of its high-strung hopes defeated by the contempt of the pagan world. Many psalms (e.g. 11, 25, 32, and especially 73) bear witness to the struggle which was the result of this painful challenge. The struggle came at last to rest in the *anawim*, the poor, who discovered that ultimately the future was God's; ultimately there was "no reason to worry about the question: what shall we eat, or what shall we drink, or what shall we have for clothing? For the pagans pursue all these things. Your Father in heaven knows that you need them. So look for his kingdom and its righteousness first, and all these things will be yours as well" (Matt. 6, 31–33).

Psalm 124

Israel may say with justice:

If God had not been for us,
when people were against us—
if God had not been for us,
we would have been eaten alive,
we would have been burnt in their rage,
the water would have sprung upon us,
the flood would have swept us away,
and in those seething waves
we would all have been lost.

But God—thanks be to him—
has saved us from their teeth.
We have escaped, like a bird
from the net of the bird-catcher.
The net is torn,
and we are flown—

Our help is the Name of the Lord,
who made the heavens and the earth.

[Psalm 124] A short hymn of thanksgiving with a liturgical beginning and using traditional imagery to express chaos and rescue. Like so many passages in the Bible, this little psalm insists on describing the attitude of faith by starting from the worst possible hypothesis: "when people were against us", a condition which in the experience of the Jews had only too often been true. In the agelong experience of Israel, however, God's help had never been conceived or proclaimed as a facile reassurance or an easy way out—from time immemorial Yahweh was known as a difficult friend. If, therefore, this psalm proclaims the freedom of Israel's Remnant from the oppression of the pagan world, it does so by alleging the Name of a God who is not only the Rock of Rescue, but also the demanding God of the patriarchs, Moses, and the prophets.—"I am convinced that the suffering of the present day is in no way comparable to the glory which is waiting to be revealed in us. For the creation, too, is yearning for the revelation of the glory of God's children. For the creation is subjected to a futile existence, not because it has wanted to, but because it was God's will that it should be so subjected. But this situation is not without hope, for the creation, too, will be delivered from its slavish subjection to destruction, to have its share in the glorious freedom of God's children" (Rom. 8. 18–21).

Psalm 126

When from our exile
God takes us home again,
that will be dreamlike.

We shall be singing,
laughing for happiness.
The world will say:
"Their God does wonders."
Yes, you do wonders,
God here among us,
you, our gladness.

Then take us home,
bring us to life,
just like the rivers
which, in the desert,
when the first rain falls
start flowing again.

Sow seed in sadness,
harvest in gladness.
A man goes his way
and sows seed with tears.
Back he comes, singing,
sheaves on his shoulder.

[Psalm 126] The history of Israel's salvation through the rescue from Egypt, her painful journey through the desert, and her occupation of the Promised Land acted as the pledges of God's continuing faithfulness. But experiences of the past, no matter how tenaciously handed on and believed, tend to harden into tales too good to be true and too far distant to be believable, unless they tally with valid experiences in the present. This is what tradition did for the great stories of Israel—it remoulded them into models of experience. The rescue from the house of slavery became the model of the life of the believer; the biblical short story (Daniel 1–6; Esther; Judith), the narrative psalms, and large portions of the wisdom-books reinforced the validity of the Exodus. This psalm, with its sapiential ending, is an example of this fusion of wisdom and generalized Exodus-spirituality.—"Amen, amen, I tell you: if the grain of wheat does not fall into the earth it remains alone; but if it dies it yields much fruit. The man who loves his life will lose it; but the man who disregards his life in this world will keep it into life eternal. If somebody wants to serve me he will have to follow me, and wherever I am, my servant will be there also. If somebody serves me, the Father will crown him with honour" (John 12. 24–26).

Psalm 127

If the Lord does not build the house,
poor builder, why go on working?
If the Lord does not guard the town,
poor watchman, your watch is in vain.

Why, then, should you get up early,—
and toil on into the night.
Your bread will still taste of sorrow.
Happiness can never be made—
the Lord gives it to his friends,
just like that, in their sleep.

Children come from God,
a son is a precious gift.
Like arrows on a man's bow
are sons born to him in his youth.
Happy is the man who has them—
he has no need to worry,
he can face up to his enemy,
he can take on the world.

[Psalms 127 and 128] These two pilgrimage hymns express the same feeling. Yahweh is present to the man who believes, and consequently he experiences the world that surrounds him not as a bare reality, but as "given", as a promise and as a challenge. Believing in God means: taking him seriously according as he can be found in the concrete situations of life—cherishing ordinary things and ordinary experiences—looking for the mystery in what you have, not in what you do not have. Happiness, in this way, comes to the believer as blessing. He experiences God's presence in a house, in a town, in labour, in strength, in a wife and children. The images of the defeat of the enemies, the olive and the vine enhance the dynamism of this experience by evoking the great themes of the Exodus.

Psalm 128

Happy is the man who
may lead his life with God.
You are that man if only
you keep his words alive.

Your hands—they will be working,
your land—it will bear fruit,
enough for you to live on.
You will be more than rich.

Your wife is a fruitful vine
that blooms in the heart of your house.
Sons, like olive branches,
are standing around your table.
In this way a man of God
knows blessing after blessing.

Receive as long as you live
all blessing from God's house,
enjoy to your heart's content
the peace of his holy city.

Be fruitful in your sons,
find blessing in their children—
thus the Lord saves his people
and gives all peace to us.

By these overtones the modest experience of human happiness is
linked up with the Covenant: the God of the Rescue gives depth to
happiness, which becomes safety, reliance, peace, trust, faith.
Psalm 128 also refers the happiness of each family to the national
happiness around the cult in the Temple.—"Is there any father
among you, who will give his son a stone when he asks for bread?
Or, if he asks for a fish, will he give him a snake instead? Or, if he
asks for an egg, will give him a scorpion? If you then, although you
are evil, are capable of giving good gifts to your children, how much
more will your Father in heaven give the holy Spirit to those who
ask him!" (Luke 11. 11–13).

Psalm 130

From the depths I am calling you, God,
Lord God, do you hear me?
Open your heart to me,
I am begging for mercy.

If you keep count of sins,
my God, who can hold his own?
But there is forgiveness
with you—your way is our life.

I expect the Lord,
I wait with all my heart—
and I hope for his word.

I look out for him,
just as a man on guard
looks out for the morning,

looks out for the morning.

Keep on trusting in God,
for there is mercy with him,
he is your redemption.

He will make us free
from the power of evil.

[Psalm 130] This intensely personal psalm sets to sound the depths of human existence in terms of guilt and forgiveness. The experience of life going on in the teeth of the destructive forces of human inadequacy and sinfulness has led the poet of this psalm to the conviction that God must be a God of forgiveness, and thus he can turn his complaint into a profession of reliance, with faith in God acting as the pivot. But faith in God is not a facile attitude—it affords no easy assurance. It is an attitude of waiting in the midst of darkness, a precarious balance between hope and fear, with hope ultimately prevailing.—"Joseph, son of David, do not fear to take Mary as your wife. The child in her womb is of the holy Spirit. She will give birth to a son whom you must call Jesus [which means: God saves], for he will make his people free from their sins" (Matt. 1. 20-21).

Psalm 131

God I am not haughty
I do not look down on others

do not imagine that I am great
do not dream enormous dreams

yes I have tamed my desires
my soul has come to rest

like a little child that has drunk
and lies at the breast of his mother

a little child that has drunk
so is my soul in me

expect everything from him
now and for evermore

[Psalm 131] This beautiful short lyric sums up the attitude of the *anawim*, the "poor". Freed from the passion for achievement and self-affirmation, reconciled to the insignificant shape of Israel after the Exile, without regrets and without disillusion, the poet of this psalm has surrendered his own limited capabilities as well as Israel's destiny to God, in the conviction that God will take care of all things, and that all things are to be found with God. "Our hearts are restless until they come to rest in You" (St Augustine).—"At that time Jesus said: 'I bless you, Father, Lord of heaven and earth, for having hidden these things from the wise and the knowing, and revealed them to children. Yes, Father, this has been your good pleasure. All things have been surrendered to me by my Father, and no one but the Father knows the Son, and no one knows the Father but the Son and any one to whom the Son chooses to reveal him. Come to me, all you who are exhausted and bent down under your burdens, and I will give you relief and rest'" (Matt. 11. 25-28).

Psalm 133

Yes, that is comfort—to live
in one house together as brothers.
It is like precious balsam,
poured out over the head
and flowing down into the beard,
the beard of Aaron, down
into the collar of his garment.
It is like the dew of Hermon,
descending on Zion's mountains.
There the Lord gives his blessing,
life in eternity.

[Psalm 133] A "Scene from Clerical Life" in the Temple at
Jerusalem: the common joy of the priests and levites is expressed
in the common pride in the attributes of their office: the oil, the
garments, the name of Aaron, and especially the height of Zion,
inconspicuous in comparison with the holy mountain of Hermon,
and yet the place of God's life-giving presence.—"All who had
come to believe formed a close unity and had everything in common.
They used to sell their property and their goods to distribute the
money among all as they needed. And day after day they met in the
Temple, faithfully and of one accord. They had the breaking of the
bread in one or other home. They enjoyed their food in joy and
simplicity of heart. They praised God. They were held in esteem by
all the people. And day after day the Lord added to their number
more people to be saved" (Acts 2. 44–47).

Psalm 137

By the streams of Babylon we sat down,
mourning at the thought of Zion.
And on the branches of the willows
that stood there we hung up our harps.

For those who had carried us away
called on us to sing a song;
our tormentors wanted something cheerful—
"Sing us one of your songs from Zion."

Ah, how should we be able to sing
of our God in a foreign land.
Jerusalem, should I ever forget you,
let me lose my right hand first.

Let my tongue turn to stone in my mouth,
if I no longer remember you,
if I do not find my greatest joy
in you, my city, Jerusalem.

O God, repay the sons of Edom
for that day when disaster came to our city—
repay those who cried: "Away with it,
let not one stone remain on another."

O city of Babylon, destroying fury,
my blessing on the man who will repay you.
My blessing on the man who seizes your children
and smashes them against the rocks.

[Psalm 137] To sing a liturgical hymn to Zion, a hymn like Psalm 46, in Babylon would be a self-defeating gesture, because the destruction of Jerusalem would seem to imply that Yahweh was no longer capable of bringing peace and prosperity to Israel. Besides, to celebrate God's presence in the territory of foreign gods would imply that after the defeat Israel's God had become one of the minor deities in the Babylonian pantheon (cf. Sennacherib's words in Is. 36. 18 ff.). And this, in turn, would be tantamount to writing off the entire history of Israel, centred around the sanctuary on Mount Zion—the playing hand and the singing tongue would be the instruments of unbelief. In this way Psalm 137 shows Israel tenaciously clinging to her faith in the teeth of an ever more meaningless *impasse*, cursing Babylon, the city of injustice and evil, and Edom, its accomplice (cf. Ezech. 35. 5–15; Obadiah 8–14), and blessing the City of God that has disappeared from sight.—"It is in faith that they all died, without having received what had been promised. But they had seen it and greeted it from afar, recognizing that they were strangers and wanderers on the earth. For people who speak thus make it clear that they are in quest of a homeland. And if in so speaking they had been thinking of the land they had left, they would have had an opportunity to return there. But actually their desire went out to a better, a heavenly country. And therefore God is not ashamed to be called their God, for he has indeed built a city for them" (Heb. 11. 13–16).

Psalm 139

My God, you fathom my heart and you know me,
my God, you know where I am, where I go.
You see through my thoughts from afar,
you have decided my roaming and resting,
and you are familiar with all that I do,
yes, and no word comes to my lips
but, my God, you have already heard it.
You are before me and you are behind me,
you have laid your hand upon me—
marvel of wisdom, far above me,
I cannot reach it, you are beyond me.

How should I ever run away from your spirit,
and where should I seek refuge—you see me everywhere.
If I climb to the heavens, you are in the heavens,
if I go into the earth, I find you there too.
And if I should fly with the day-break
down to the uttermost shore of the sea,
there also your hand will help me on,

there also your powerful hand holds me tight.
If I should cry: "Darkness, cover me,
let the night come down round about me"—
for you the darkness does not exist,
for you the night is as bright as the day,
the darkness is as clear as the light.
I am your creation in my bones and tissues,
you have woven me in the womb of my mother.
I thank you, you have so wonderfully made me,
awesome wonders are all your works.
I am known by you, to the core, to my soul—
nothing in me was hidden from your eyes
when I was fashioned in deepest secrecy,
beautifully twined in the womb of the earth.
I was still unborn—you had already seen me,
and all of my life was in your book
before one day of it had been shaped.

How difficult are your thoughts to me,
my God, what a world of wisdom!
Were I to count them, they are as numerous
as the sand on the seashore, and yet—
I still know nothing at all about you.

God, kill the man with wicked plans—
away from me, people with blood on your hands.
They speak of you, but mean to discredit you,
they use your name, but only to betray you.
Should I not hate, God, those who hate you,
not be sick at heart over those who oppose you?
I hate them as fiercely as I can hate,
from now on they are my own enemies.

Now fathom my heart, o God, and know me,
test me and know what is happening in me.
I shall not come to a dead end, shall I?
Lead me forward on the way of my fathers.

[Psalm 139] One of the classical elements of supplication is a profession of innocence, often accompanied by an indignant denunciation of the unrighteous; a prayer like Psalm 26 is even wholly based on this pattern. As, however, the awareness of God's transcendence was more explicitly explored, Israel became ever more sensitive to the precariousness of protestations of innocence: who can fathom the depths of his own heart, and who knows his own secret evil (cf. Ps. 19. 11–13)? For the poet of Psalm 139 this question leads to a dreadful ambiguity. He is faced with a God whose fearful presence does not even let a man swallow his own spittle in peace (cf. Job 7. 19), but who is also the God of Psalm 8, the God whose heart is touched by the thought of Man. No wonder, then, that his protestation of innocence sticks in his throat, and that the close of his impressive poem is not the simple affirmation: "Your mercy is before my eyes, and I lead my life in your truth" (Ps. 26. 3). On the contrary, it is a surrender to the inscrutable scrutiny of a God whose faithfulness is as reliable as it is mysterious.—"The word of God is alive and active, sharper than any two-edged sword. It penetrates to the point of contact of soul and spirit, of joints and marrow, and discerns the deepest thoughts and intentions of man. No creature is hidden from him, but everything is open and laid bare before his eyes. It is with him that we have to do" (Heb. 4. 12–13).

Psalm 142

I am crying out, I cry to God—
o God, I implore you and beg for mercy.

I pour out my troubles before his eyes,
I pour out my whole heart to him.

I can go no further, I am out of breath—
but you, you know a way out for me.

They have set traps and snares on my way,
whichever way I turn, no friend,

no friend for me, no refuge any more,
no one who cares for me in the least.

I cried out to you, o God, I called:
my refuge, you, my all in this life.

But listen then, I am almost dead,
save me then, they are after me, they are too much for me.

They are hemming me in, God, get me out of this,
and I will show you how grateful I am.

And all your friends will wish me joy,
because you have been good to me.

[Psalm 142] This psalm is a classical specimen of the complaint. Starting from a description of the situation of someone wrongly persecuted, it turns into a desperate prayer, and looks forward to the atmosphere of relief and gladness around the thanksgiving sacrifice when the trial is over. The Hebrew Bible attributes this psalm "to David, when he was in the cave", the prototypical situation of the just man called by God and hounded down by his enemies (cf. I Sam. 22. 1; 24. 1–7), whom he refuses to attack because he trusts in God.—"You have heard that the Law says: 'An eye for an eye, and a tooth for a tooth.' But I tell you not to resist injustice. But if anyone strikes you on the right cheek, turn to him the other also. And if anyone wants to take you to court in order to get your coat, let him have your cloak as well. And if anyone forces you to go one mile, go with him two miles"(Matt. 5. 38–41).

Psalm 147

1

A song of praise to the Lord,
singing makes you happy,
singing to our God,
for he is pleased with psalms.

He builds a city of peace
for the people of his covenant.
However far we are scattered,
he calls us together again.

Broken people are healed,
and he binds up their wounds,
our God, who defines again,
every night, the number of the stars,

who calls them all by name—
a powerful God is he,
this God of ours—and his wisdom
is great beyond all measure.

He helps the poor man up,
he brings pride to a fall.
We must sing in praise of his Name,
we have to make music for him,

who covers the heavens with clouds
and makes the rain for the earth,
who clothes the mountains in green
and gives the animals their food—

and even the fledgling raven
gets what he cries out for.
No, he does not care
for horsepower or iron muscles,

his heart goes out to those
who are waiting for his love,
his friends in hope and fear—
and so he is our God.

II

Jerusalem, city of God,
people, glorify him.
He has safely barred your gates,
he has given your children his blessing.

He gives you bread and peace—
you live a life of abundance.
He sends his word to the earth,
and it runs, it spreads like wildfire.

And sometimes he makes it snow,
a white and woolly fur,
he scatters hoar-frost like ashes,
and hail-showers, stones of ice.

Who can endure his cold?
But then he speaks a word—
it thaws, the wind is blowing,
the waters are flowing again.

To Jacob and to his house
he has entrusted his word,
his law, his revelation,
his covenant and promise.

There is no other people
that may so experience him,
that may so keep his words—
our song rings to high heaven.

[Psalm 147] This psalm, which the Vulgate divides into two separate psalms, is a very poetical summary of the discoveries which Israel was led to make in the course of its history. It is full of memories and quotations from the prophetic writings before, during, and after the Exile, and from the book of Job. God is the Rescuer of Israel who is also the Creator of the world. He is the God of the poor, the friend of the helpless, whom he gathers around his city of peace in order to make himself known to them. The peculiar charm of this poem lies in the fact that the awe of God, the Creator, has been interiorized and incorporated into the modest joy of the believing community that feels at home with its God.—"Life is more than food, and the body is more than clothing. Look at the ravens—they neither sow nor mow, they have neither storehouse nor barn, and yet God feeds them. How much more are you than the birds! And for that matter, who among you can add one cubit to his span of life by worrying? If, then, you are powerless in such a small matter, why do you worry about the rest? Think of the flowers, how they grow—they neither spin nor weave. Yet I tell you, even Solomon in all his splendour was not arrayed like any one of them. But if God so clothes the plants in the fields, alive today and thrown into the oven tomorrow, how much more will be clothe you, men of little faith!" (Luke 12. 23–28).

Psalm 149

Halleluiah,
a new song for the Lord our God.
Sing to him,
he has called you all together.
Israel
must be glad for the sake of her maker,
Zion's children
must revel and shout for joy for their King.
Dance to him
as a tribute to his Name,
strike up music
on your kettledrums and harps.
Our God
has chosen a people for himself.
He redeems,
he brings to greatness humble people.
All his friends
may glory and take a pride in him,
nights on end
they may acclaim and worship him.

From their mouths
comes a hymn of praise to the Lord,
in their hands
the two-edged sword is eagerly flashing.
So they will
execute his revenge on the peoples,
punishment
across the shoulders of the nations.
And their rulers—
they will tie them fast and shackle them,
powers that be—
they will put them in chains and fetters.

So they will
carry out his law and his sentence.
So God gives
glory and honour to all his friends.
Halleluiah.

[Psalm 149] As the Jews had to cope with the problem of oppression they came to reassert their faith in God's rescue in terms of a
belief in the ultimate victory of God's chosen people over their
enemies, just as the decline of the monarchy produced the image
of the ideal king at the end of time (cf. Ps. 72). During the last few
centuries B.C. the proclamation of this ultimate victory, rooted in
the prophetic tradition (cf., e.g., Is. 60–66; Ezech. 25–28), took the
shape of apocalyptic literature: the book of Daniel (which the Greek
Bible was to expand and count as one of the great prophets) is a
brilliant effort to come to terms with the disintegration of the
Jewish nation under the oppression of the pagan world, by pointing
to the final restoration of justice and righteousness on the ruins of
the powers that be. In the dream-world of the apocalyptic writings
historic personages and events loom large in and out of context,
imaginary characters and hosts of angels join in a cosmic struggle
between light and darkness, God's hidden plans are revealed by
means of allusion, symbolic numbers, oracles and meaningful
events—all with the purpose of encouraging the humiliated be-
lievers not to give up faith and hope. This holy conviction about the
victory of the righteous, however, also found a rather more down-
to-earth and realistic expression in stories such as the rescue of
Daniel from the lions' den (Dan. 6), and above all in the penny
novels of Judith and Esther, with their strong appeal to popular
chauvinism. Psalm 149, militant, chauvinistic, and visionary,
illustrates the fervour as well as the ambiguity of Jewish eschato-
logy.—"Halleluiah! Salvation and glory and power belong to our
God, for his judgments are true and just. He has condemned the
great harlot who ruined the earth with her harlotry. He has avenged
on her the blood of his servants. Halleluiah!" (Apoc. 19. 1–3).

Psalm 150

Praise the Lord in his holy house,
the firmament of his majesty.
Praise him for his powerful works,
praise him, he is immeasurably great.

Praise him with your resounding horns,
and with your lutes and harps and guitars.
Praise him with dancing and tambourines,
tune your strings and play the flute.

Praise him with kettledrums and cymbals,
brass and woodwind, a choir of voices,
halleluiah, shouts of joy,
all the living are praising the Lord.

[Psalm 150] Psalm 150 is the final doxology, the epilogue of the book of psalms. It sums up its character by summing up the character of the cult: the liturgical evocation of God's glory, present in the midst of the community. It was in the liturgy that Israel celebrated her coming to life as the community whose faith in God was founded upon the rescue from Egypt, the social and religious experiences in the desert, and the entry into Canaan (cf., e.g., the liturgical prayers in Deut. 26). It was in the liturgy, too, that this original core was developed: the repeated proclamation of the Covenant permitted Israel to view her subsequent history as well as the traditions about what lay before the Exodus as ever so many manifestations of God's abiding faithfulness, and thus, as being vitally connected with the Exodus. In this way the history and sensibility of Israel was accompanied by a steady flow of liturgy, which articulated and interpreted the present by re-enacting the past. It is not surprising, then, that—when the fullest available traditions about Israel's desert experiences were recorded (Exod. 1–Num. 24)–they were clustered around a highly dramatic, "prototypical" account of the most solemn moments of the Temple liturgy, set on Mount Sinai (Exod. 19. 9–25), with the blast of the horn evoking the presence of God as its culminating point. Psalm 150 expresses Israel's faith in a liturgy feeding into life and fed into by life, just as the account of the Sinai liturgy served as a literary expedient to lend present relevance to past facts.—"Let your hearts be ruled by the peace of Christ, to which you were indeed called as members of the one body. And be grateful. Let the word of Christ live among you abundantly. Teach and admonish one another with all wisdom. And with grateful heart sing to God psalms, hymns, and songs inspired by the Spirit. And whatever you do, in word or deed, do everything in the name of Jesus, the Lord, giving thanks to God the Father through him" (Col. 3. 15–17).

Index to First Lines

A NOTE ON THE AUTHORSHIP OF THIS BOOK

In the course of 1967 the model, and in many ways the original, of the present book appeared in the Netherlands under the title *Vijftig Psalmen, Proeve van een nieuwe vertaling*. It was the result of a close collaboration of two poets, Huub Oosterhuis and Michel van der Plas, with two exegetes, Pius Drijvers and Han Renckens. The psalms in that collection were translated into English by Frans Jozef van Beeck in collaboration with David Smith and Forrest Ingram. The introduction is largely based on an article by Han Renckens, published in the catechetical review *Verbum* under the title "Vijftig Psalmen", translated by David Smith, and adapted for the present book by Frans Jozef van Beeck, who also wrote the commentaries on the psalms.